NO SECOND CHANCE

Martin Tierney

No Second Chance
REFLECTIONS OF A DUBLIN PRIEST

the columba press

First published in 2010 by
the columba press
55A Spruce Avenue, Stillorgan Industrial Park,
Blackrock, Co Dublin

Cover by Bill Bolger
Origination by The Columba Press
Printed in Ireland by ColourBooks Ltd, Dublin

ISBN 978 1 85607 701 9

Copyright © 2010, Martin Tierney

Contents

Foreword — 7
Introduction — 9

PART ONE: THE ROAD TO PRIESTHOOD

1. The Historical Background — 15
2. School — 18
3. Seminary — 22
4. Light and Darkness — 27
5. Learning Philosophy and Theology — 34
6. Seminary Spirituality — 41

PART TWO: ON BEING A PRIEST

7. Ordination — 51
8. Archbishop McQuaid — 60
9. The Parish — 66
10. The Dead and the Dying — 80
11. Sex Abuse — 84

Foreword

First appearances are always deceptive. In a world of instant media we have answers before the questions have come off the press. We seldom have time to ask 'Why?'

This book was written to try and put together some of the mysteries of the Irish Catholic church's recent past. Why was the inordinate emphasis on obedience driven to the extremes of physical violence? Why was a system of physical and psychological coercion used to deprive people of their willingness and ability to think?

Real questions have seldom been asked about acts in which we participated willingly. We allowed a system to diminish others without ever shouting stop.

Why was authority abused? Authority is an act of service and Jesus gave us so many examples in his own life of going out to serve people. One could hardly compare the church of the 1950s with the Jesus of the gospels. I lived through this period and most of my life was engulfed by the church, its words and its influences and yet I did little.

This book is a very small attempt to set the record straight. It is my effort in saying sorry, not just for all those of my age group who were in positions of authority, but for quietly acquiescing in what every right thinking person must have known was wrong.

I especially offer this book to those men who courageously left the priesthood or abandoned their studies having seen the light of the gospel of Jesus. They left seminaries when it was an act of extreme courage. They have been ignored by the church for so long. It is time to thank them and invite them to join with us in taking part in a renewal that will be much more than a return to the past.

Introduction

January 14th was dull and grey that Sunday morning in 2001. The Christmas frenzy had left people drained. Little was happening in the city. People slept late. Traffic lights changed futilely. While the city slumbered, in one church an elderly priest knelt before his bishop to be installed as Parish Priest of a parish in the southern suburbs of the Dublin. Now nearly forty years ordained, he was about 5 feet nine in height, of slim build, with the worry lines of years just beginning to crease his forehead. At sixty-two years of age, a time when most of his contemporaries had retired, he was about to accept a primary responsibility within the Catholic Church. It was twenty-two years since he had last worked in a parish.* He was apprehensive. His misgivings were solidly grounded in the seismic changes that had happened since he last worked in a parish. A paradigm shift in the cultural and religious landscape of Ireland had left in its wake a puzzled, confused and uncertain congregation. The change was as great as the discovery by some primitive Amazonian tribe that a sophisticated world of technology existed beyond their tribal land.

He could remember that his feelings related comfortably to the little 'whiskey priest,' of Graham Green's novel, *The Power and the Glory:*

> He was a man who was supposed to save souls. It had seemed quite simple once, preaching at Benediction, organising the guilds, having coffee with elderly ladies behind

---

* His priestly ministry had varied from early parochial appointments in Glasnevin, Walkinstown and Swords, to a period of nearly twenty-five years in non-parochial appointments with The Charismatic Renewal, The Catholic Communications Institute and a variety of other positions, before returning now to parochial life.

barred windows, blessing new houses with a little incense, wearing black gloves. It was as easy as saving money: now it was a mystery. He was aware of his desperate inadequacy.

He was worried about his ability to work effectively in the changed environment.

The huge cavernous church, built to hold twelve hundred people, echoed as the bishop's voice bounced off the large empty galleries. Thirty years previously it had been packed with people. They sweated in the heat of bodies pressed together. The bishop handed over the keys of the church intoning, 'Receive these keys, guard and protect your church and watch over the flock that has been entrusted to you.' The priest responded, 'I undertake to work faithfully in the care of this parish and all its people, and to promote the best interests of the parishioners.'

The elderly congregation had seen priests come and ago. Why should this one be any different?. They too had lived through the glory days when an All-Ireland football final at Croke Park was preceded by the singing of *Faith of Our Fathers*. They had doffed their hats to priests and kissed bishops' rings and fasted from midnight to receive the Eucharist. Now they were rocked at the collapse of a world that had comforted them. As the priest rose, the words of the bishop were still fresh, 'At all times let your life be an example of Christ's compassion and care for his people. Seek to know and cherish these brothers and sisters of the Lord.' There was pathos about a scene that formerly would have been the focus of gossip within the community. 'What is the new Parish Priest like?' would have engaged the conversation of most of the parishioners. Now only a very small percentage of the people cared. Worse was still to come. Little did either bishop or priest know that a crisis, this time of clerical sex abuse, was about to break over the Catholic Church in Ireland like an unrestrained tidal wave. Both had coped reasonably well with the loss of power and respect. Neither the priest, nor the bishop, knew their breaking point. This is a story, not about me, although I will use the experiences and events of my life as scaffolding from which to explore the events that shaped the New Ireland from a religious perspective.

We had a childhood game that involved being blindfolded

by companions. The blindfold was securely tightened to exclude every trace of light or possibility of vision. After being twirled around several times to ensure disorientation, the blindfolded one was let loose to try and identify a person in the room by feel and touch only. Ears, noses, lips and mouths, were sensitively probed for glimmers of a clue. Wild guesses were shouted out to shrieks of laughter, especially when gender was mistaken. Height was one big give-away. It was a twilight world of fun. I still live in the word of blind-man's buff. Nothing is certain. Living by feel and touch, and probing for the truth, has become a way of life. At that time, sixty long years ago, the world of the blindfold was paradoxically a world of clarity. Everything had its place. Values and beliefs were rarely questioned or tested. There was innocence; some would call it naïveté, about our stance towards life. But that was it.

My world then, in a grim post-war Ireland, was a world of turf and cod liver oil. It was a world of rules. No dancing after midnight. No meat on Fridays. No work on Sundays. No food before the Eucharist. No answering back. Don't go into Protestant churches. The scrutinising of the minutiae of every action with a view to determining where it stood on the Richter scale of sinfulness was common. Hell, with the smell of burning flesh, was never far away. Arriving there was a distinct possibility. This was not to say that there wasn't gaiety and fun. Of course there was. There were summers when the sun always shone. Tadpoles were collected in jam jars, and rickety tree houses were built as secret hideouts.

PART ONE

The Road to Priesthood

CHAPTER ONE

The Historical Background

It was a world of obedience. Obey whatever the cost. Don't argue. Father knows best. Do what you are told. Be seen but not heard. Believe without understanding. Elders are always right. They had the wisdom that would your ensure safety and security, or so we were told. Others did our thinking for us. Parents, church, teacher, were the arbiters of behaviour that brooked no opposition. The motto, like the Crimean volunteer, was, 'Theirs not to reason why, theirs but to do and die'

The fledgling state had contracted, as it were, a *marriage de convenance*, with the 'bride of Christ', the Roman Catholic Church. What seems strange to us now was then considered virtually of divine ordinance. A marriage made in heaven. It may even have been the church that wore the trousers! For the most part, for reasons of expediency, the arrangement worked to the advantage of both. The gombeen men of means also had a long-term flirtation with the church. They had the money, the church had the power, and they needed one another. Gerard O'Donovan brilliantly portrays this latter fact in the biographical novel, *Father Ralph*.

There were figures in my youth who didn't obey. The Tailor and Ansty would never be etched in folklore had they not stepped out of line. Peadar O'Donnell, a fiery socialist, was always squaring up to the powerful pockets of vested interests. Dan Breen, the gnarled revolutionary gunman, stubbornly refused to be reconciled to the church. Noel Browne, a querulous dissident by nature, always made headlines. I even heard of a priest who had left the ministry, by the name of Boyd-Barrett. I also dimly remember the brouhaha over a play *The Rose Tattoo* and the arrest of its director Alan Simpson. These were exceptions. Arty people didn't count as they had a licence to be different. Apart from these disturbing people, the Catholic Church reinforced the *status quo* in the national psyche. These people were heroes. Their rebellious or courageous streak placed them outside the pale of respectability. That's the way they wanted it.

The church was a potent force in maintaining the *status quo*. At eighty year of age an old uncle of mine, born at the beginning of the twentieth century, recalled with sadness, hearing the name of a girl who was pregnant outside marriage, being read from the altar in the parish of Kilfenora. Such a pregnancy spelled banishment. The church had at its disposal a trained cadre of clerics who would maintain discipline and rigid orthodoxy. I lived unquestioning in this world for over half a lifetime. It's gone. Was it a mirage? A world of illusion? Or was it 'the good old days' that we need to return to?

Over the years, in the leap from the 'Emergency,' as the Second World War was called in Ireland, to digital TV, the family began to change. It loosened up and became less hierarchical. Young people were listened to more and more. They became part of the family decision-making process. The nuclear family based on marriage was no longer the only acceptable form of family structure. Most profoundly the church changed. Paradoxically, it changed utterly and it remained obstinately the same. Janus-like it is facing in two directions at the same time, forward and backwards. This, in a way, is why I am still in the world of blind man's buff. Still trying to feel the shape of things and make sense of them. To my understanding, the truth is not exclusively to be found under the cupola of St Peter's. It may be there, but it is also within oneself. It is also within and without the community of believers. Who can put boundaries on the truth or where it is to be found?

This book is an honest analysis of my experience of church over forty years of priesthood, but it is not an autobiography in the strict sense. Perish the thought! I suppose it is chic to denigrate the past. Human nature doesn't change that much. We can learn from our past especially from our mistakes. There are deep chasms of difference in the Roman Catholic Church today. It is not unlike Irish republicans, who split and split again, each group maintaining itself to be the sole inheritors of the legacy of the Second Dáil of 1922, which all claimed had never been properly dissolved.

THE HISTORICAL BACKGROUND

That is not the way it was when I was born on 28 December 1938. My father, Martin, came from Caheramore near Kilfenora, Co Clare. My grandmother, Ellen, was a widow for fifty years and raised a family of nine on a small holding of poor land. She was probably illiterate. This didn't exclude her from a depth of wisdom, especially in the manner in which she guided her family towards successful lives. My mother Joan, nee Russell, came from Rathgar and a family of thirteen. It was said that her father had been, for a short time, secretary to Charles Stuart Parnell. She had two brother priests. One, the Parish Priest of Totnes in Devon, grew very close to Sean O'Casey in later years. The other, a Redemptorist, was Director of the Arch-Confraternity in Limerick. Another brother, Charles, was one of those responsible for the establishment of the Irish Air Corps and was in London ready to fly Collins home if the Treaty negotiations broke down in December 1921. During the Civil War, with Major McSwiney, he flew many reconnaissance missions against the Irregulars. One uncle, also a member of the Irish Air Corps in its early years, crashed in his plane and died. In a poem written in his memory, Oliver St John Gogarty captured his dashing character. I have three sisters, Hilda, Mary and Clare (deceased) and one brother John.

In my early youth, truth was handed down. Today it is searched for. I am on a journey of discovery. My views, which many readers will disagree with, are naturally coloured by my present position on that journey. I do not intend to look back all the time but, like the church, to look back and forward. What does the future hold? What resources spiritual and personal do we have to effect change? I try to use the experiences of my life to tease out the lessons I have learned. I hope they may be provocative, irritating, truthful, honest and helpful.

CHAPTER TWO

School

'Hang a Jesuit,' says a Spanish proverb, 'and he'll make off with the rope.' In the Jesuits, the church had 'Green Berets' of Christendom. The mission statement of one would almost have fitted the other.

The creed of the US Marines reads:

> I am an American soldier
> I will always place my mission first.
> I will never accept defeat.
> I will never quit.
> I will never leave a fallen comrade.
> I am an American soldier.
> I live by this creed.

In Protestant legend Ignatius Loyola, the founder of the Jesuits, is an ogre who master-minded the Counter Reformation. One writer claimed that 'it was an evil day for new-born Protestantism when a French artilleryman fired the shot that struck down Ignatius Loyola ... the soldier gave himself to a new warfare. In the forge of his great intellect, heated but not disturbed by the intense fire of zeal, was wrought the prodigious enginery whose power has been felt to the uttermost confines of the world.'[1] A maxim traditionally applied to the Jesuits, but probably apocryphal, says 'Give me the child for the first seven years, and you can do what you like with him afterwards.' I spent ten years with the Jesuits and I do believe they did things with me that others couldn't.

The Jesuits had the learning and ingenuity, not so much to change water into wine, but to produce from the dullest material someone capable of succeeding. The Jesuit education I received in the 1950s, firstly at Belvedere College and later at Clongowes, weaselled out of me the areas where I had some potential ability.

SCHOOL

As a generally mediocre student, without a passion for higher learning, the Jesuits worked on the material presented. They were good at fostering talent, especially in those with little interest in or aptitude for academic study. Their stance towards education was holistic. Musical appreciation, drama, art appreciation, debating, were a natural part of the curriculum. Knowing the difference between a fugue and a sonata, or a chord and an arpeggio, or the basics of composition in painting, did add a breath of vision in the life of a young person. I well remember my first introduction to Beethoven's Pastoral Symphony, when we were told by a passionate lover of music, T. C. Kelly, that 'Here, we have both painting and mood-evocation, and the latter not the former is the source of the music lover's chief delight.' Tom Ryan taught appreciation of painting. From him I learned that, 'the position of the artist is humble. He is essentially a channel.'

Filing into the school debating society on a Monday night and speaking impromptu for three minutes on a previously unknown topic sharpened the mind. This sort of training is one of the reasons why I have always found it difficult to use a script when preaching. I also had the privilege of having playwright Tom McIntyre as my teacher of English and History. These two subjects ignited in me a life-long thirst for reading and an interest in the past. Tom was a short-back-and-sides man then. His infectious love of literature couldn't be resisted. Religious education I found challenging. I experienced being constantly stretched in class, especially when grappling with subjects like St Thomas Aquinas's five proofs for the existence of God. Hart's *Christian Doctrine* presented a confrontation with faith and mystery. Drama, music, and debating these were the Jesuits' forte. I revelled in all these pursuits. An added bonus was a swim before Mass and breakfast, even on dark winter days.

The priests invariably treated us with respect. Corporal punishment was administered by use of a thick leather strap called a 'pandy bat'. However, a 'cheque system', meant that only certain priests or scholastics were 'licensed' to wield the bat, thereby ensuring that the injured party was seldom the one to administer the punishment. The cancelled cheque, duly stamped, was returned as proof that the victim had received his due rewards!

The usual punishment for serious misdemeanours was 'six of the best', which were called 'biffs' in Greyfriaresque language, no doubt a throwback to the English Public School system. It all reminds me now of Mr Quelch, master of the Remove, the *eminence grise* of poor old Billy Bunter and his friend Bob Cherry. A final physical sanction was available in the armoury of corporal punishment. This unsavoury punishment went by the name of 'cockers'. It entailed the indignity of removing one trousers and receiving your assigned quota of 'biffs' on the bare buttocks. This type of punishment was seriously questionable as it appeared to me to have grave undertones of sexual gratification.

I always had a high tolerance for pain. None of the punishment I received, and at one time I had thick blood-filled welts on the palms of my hands, made any difference. It is hard to change the spirit through inflicting punishment on the body. Punishment didn't make me resentful. I was rarely punished unfairly. But corporal punishment is sterile. Its intention was to effect a change of behaviour. In my case, it failed lamentably. At that time there didn't seem to be any more creative way of encouraging academic learning than the pandy bat. When corporal punishment was phased out, its substitute of writing lines was equally sterile. There are schools where transcribing the telephone directory, or the school rules, are imposed as punishment. When my father promised me a bicycle if I managed to get into the first seven in class, I succeeded. Incentive driven encouragement is far more productive than physical punishment.

Religion was important in Clongowes, but I can never recall feeling pressurised. We had an annual three-day retreat. One enduring memory is a retreat given us by Fr Tom Counihan SJ, who began in a deep booming voice: 'It is appointed unto man once to die and after death the judgement.' I had never seen a dead person nor had any of my relatives died. Death was a foreign country. However, the religious tenor of the times was gilded by fear which naturally kept most Catholics in check. We were lucky to have a deeply spiritual man, Fr Kevin McDowell, as our spiritual director who was invariably kept busy. Kevin later returned to the diocesan priesthood and died as the Parish Priest of Harold's Cross. Some of the priests and the lay masters togged out and played football with the school boys. Such fraternisation would have been frowned on in the seminary.

Games were an important part of the school's curriculum. Rugby, tennis, swimming and cricket were the main sports, for which 'colours' were awarded, to those who made the school team. 'Colours' boys wore a different coloured blazer on Sunday's. I loved games and tried hard, but was never more than a 'seconds' man. I made the school swimming team regularly, but the best I achieved was third in a Leinster championship. In winter, rugby was compulsory. In my year, a group of academically inclined students held poetry readings, with raised umbrellas, close enough to the playing field to be deemed participants in the game taking place nearby. Cricket was also compulsory in the summer term. There was too much 'hanging around' in cricket for me to take it seriously. To be surrounded by hundreds of acres of meadows and woodland and playing fields, was a real privilege, which I think I was conscious of at the time. The relationships established in a boarding school are solid and lasting and contributed greatly to the experience of school.

What did the Jesuits do for me? They gave me self-belief. They taught me how to go on teaching myself for the rest of my life. One old Belvederian wrote that, 'A Jesuit education is a long fuse that detonates a gratifying explosion of erudition in later years.' I believe this was true in my case. It amazed me that so many of my colleagues, both in Belvedere and Clongowes, not academically inclined at school, were extraordinarily successful in later life. They passed on to us a 'can-do' ethic that gave us the courage to try anything.

CHAPTER THREE

Seminary

Is thirty years after ordination too late to discover why one became a priest? In 1959 when I entered the seminary, being a priest meant helping others and I wanted to do that – or so I thought. Dressing up and offering Mass must have been an enticement. I am an enthusiast by nature, and my schools days were filled with stories of the heroic deeds of the early Jesuits. Their feast days were festive occasions in the school calendar. We called them 'play days'. St Francis Xavier, who died on the island of Shang Hwan, near the mouth of the Canton in 1552 while waiting for a Chinese junk to put him secretly ashore on mainland China, was a spiritual kamikaze – utterly committed and fearless. St Isaac Jogues, who was tomahawked by Indians in 1645, was the first white man to reach the eastern entrance of Lake Superior in Canada. St Ignatius of Loyola, the founder of the Jesuits, was the author of one of the most famous books in all of Catholicism – *The Spiritual Exercises*. St Aloysius Gonzaga, the Jesuit novice, caught a fever nursing the sick. Fr Willie Doyle was a Great War army chaplain who, in the middle of winter, was reputed as a penance to stand up to his neck in the pond at Rathfarnham Castle! I was inspired by their lives. I had heard Frank Duff, the founder of the Legion of Mary, say 'We are all called to be saints.' Yes, that is what I wanted – or so I thought. Would that it was as simple as that. Nevertheless, I do believe that I, and those who entered Clonliffe College, the Dublin Diocesan Seminary, with me, had the will to holiness, which for us probably meant trying to get and remain close to God.

I waited thirty years for a measure of clarity on why I choose the priesthood. It happened far from home. The foothills of the Sange de Christo Mountains in New Mexico rise about 7,000 feet above sea level and overlook a sinuous, rolling terrain of mesas, buttes, valleys, and canyons. These foothills are the home to

SEMINARY

artists, tourists, 'New Agers,' Native Americans, and coyotes. I spent one hundred days there seeking not merely renewal, but a refoundation of my priesthood. I went to the Sangre de Christo Centre in New Mexico in 1994. On the very first day we were asked to do a life-line. Over a period of a few days we were helped to draw from our life's experience all the important events, both positive and negative, from our first conscious moment on planet earth. Everything we could remember was to be documented. This was the unrefined raw material of the next 100 days. It was explosively self-revelatory. It spoke to me of who I was and what had shaped me

My father, a very successful bank manager, demanded excellence. Failure was a word absent from his vocabulary. I have never discovered whether I was simply stupid, lazy, or just indifferent to academic achievement. I knew I never measured up to my father's expectation of what a son of his ought to be. Even the brutal physical beatings I received failed to spur me to anything other than mediocrity. Where I couldn't excel I didn't compete. It was incomprehensible to my father that I was acutely dyslexic where mathematics was concerned. I was a failure. When my school report came home he would stand me in front him and say in an utterly exasperated tone of voice, 'Imagine a line of twenty three boys and a Tierney third from the end? You're a disgrace. Go up to your room!' Punishment, in the form of a severe beating, would follow. It was of little consolation to him that I might have got first place in my class in English and third in History.

My lack of academic success led to all sorts of deviousness on my part. When in Belevedere, I was usually first into school, hopefully, to copy my 'themes' (the name given to homework) from another student. I became adept at steaming open my school report and changing ones into sevens or fours, or adding a nought where it was to my advantage. Re-sealing the envelope was the tricky part! On one occasion I received a big round nought in geometry. I think that was the cause of my leaving Belvedere. My father enquired how I managed to get nought! The response from the school was that I had copied at the examination. This wasn't true. I got on the number ten bus at Donnybrook and all the way to Findlater's Church on Parnell

Square, I studied three theorems. Imagine my utter amazement when I opened the examination paper to find the three theorems I had studied staring quizzically at me. It was like Christmas and my birthday all rolled up together. Needless to say, I reproduced the theorems exactly as they were in the text book. I was damned by my reputation and what was considered convincing circumstantial evidence! In the words of Walter Scott, 'O what a tangled web we weave, when first we practise to deceive.' I still remember the theorems, which were about 'medians'. What a median actually is still escapes me!

The only way I could win my father's approval was to achieve something that he considered very important. He had a simple faith. His early environment was steeped in the faith of the Roman Catholic Church. Even the cattle were Catholics! Each morning on his way to work, he invariably stopped to visit a church and light a candle. The sacraments and regular attendance at Mass were not optional in our house. A priest in the family was something of which my father would be immensely proud. Looking back, although I have no recollection of it at the time, I am convinced that I became a priest to win my father's approval. I cannot recall my mother having a significant influence on me. She was in the background, doggedly fighting her corner against a man whose aggression, I believe, stemmed from feelings of his own inadequacy. When I was ordained my father was tremendously proud. I had finally won his favour! Did that mean I was unhappy at my discovery thirty years later of my father's role in my vocation? No. The mixed motives for becoming a priest included this, but also many other tangled thoughts and desires. I loved people and wanted to be of service. I thought I could make the world a better place. I had a heart for preaching the word of God and felt it was a talent I had waiting to be developed. I must have felt God was calling and I made the choice to follow. The whole thing was a bit like an arranged marriage. With the twenty/twenty vision of hindsight, the figure of my father loomed large.

My elder sister Hilda was a boarder at Dominican Convent, Wicklow. My brother John was also a boarder at Clongowes. I left the year he arrived. We were birds of passage in each other's company. To some extent our lives lacked the intimacy that might have been reached had we lived together through adolescence. Thankfully, as adults we have drawn closer together. My sister Mary, who was seriously ill in her youth, was always a day pupil. One of the most devastating experiences of my life was when my father and mother came to visit me at school. They brought me to Lawlor's Hotel in Naas and said they had something serious to confide to me. Clare, my youngest sister, who was two years of age at the time, was Down's Syndrome. She was being placed with the Daughters of Charity and wouldn't be living at home any more. I was numb with confusion and my mind brimmed over with unanswered questions. I was distraught by the news.

I was trained, religiously speaking, into an Ireland with a surfeit of priests. Not long before I was ordained there was insufficient work for the priests ordained at home. Many had to go abroad until positions became available. Young men were being turned away from their home seminaries in Wexford, Kilkenny, Carlow and Waterford and even Maynooth. Many sought admittance to Holy Cross College, Clonliffe Road, and the seminary for Dublin, which I entered in 1958. We were told if we wished to leave there were many others waiting to take our place.

I entered the diocesan seminary on 11 September 1959. Holy Cross College Clonliffe is located on Clonliffe Road, Drumcondra, just off the main road from the city to the Airport. At that time there were one hundred and nine students studying at the College. All were destined for work in the Diocese of Dublin. I joined a class of seventeen. The now empty edifice sits uneasily in the shadow of the mighty new GAA stadium at Croke Park. Clonliffe was built on the former Grange of St Mary's Abbey, whose Chapter House still exists at Meeting House Lane, off Capel St, in the heart of Dublin. The well known street names in the locality – Abbey St and Mary St – harken back to this twelfth-century monastic foundation. In a letter to Dr Croke, dated 5 August 1876, Cardinal Cullen, the founder of the College, wrote: 'The land of Clonliffe is according to the best authorities the place where the Battle of Clontarf, fought on Good Friday 1014, was concluded.' *The Irish Builder* of 1860 and 1861, said of the proposed building:

The exterior will be of plain and massive character, cornices and string courses of granite will mark the separation of the storeys. A large central projection and projections on the wings will divide the façade into three portions. In the central portion only, the windows will have heavy stone dressing. With the exception of granite quoins the entire surface will be plain.

The College was opened in 1863.

CHAPTER THREE

Light and Darkness

I felt apprehensive, uneasy, and slightly out of place in this strange environment. It was like the time I went caving near Lisdoonvarna. I squeezed into a wet suit and helmet. Then, crawling like a slug on my belly, I squashed into a hole from which a stream was flowing. After a painful wriggle I found myself in a huge spooky cavern. I was enveloped by darkness with only the pencil-slim light from my helmet showing me the way. This was a strange intimidating world. When the gate closed behind the new seminarian, what was called 'the world' was consigned to a reservoir of memories. But we brought all our baggage with us. In a previous life we had indentured ourselves to 'worldly' things that remained with us, even if only in our minds and hearts. We straddled two worlds. We counted the days on our calendars until the next holiday, just as I had done in boarding school. We were hardly seeking that 'chastity of the mind' that demanded a cutting of former ties like the severing the umbilical cord of a newly born baby. As we entered Clonliffe, the interior battle in the desert of the mind, that is a prelude to holiness, was well below the horizon of our consciousness. We knew nothing of doing battle with our interior demons. All that would come later. I suspect that for most of us it came well after ordination.

I don't think I was ever really happy. I could never live up to my own idealism. By constantly falling short of the goals I set I became a bit dispirited.

We all adopted a new clerical garb. A long black serge dress-like garment called a soutane. A biretta, which was a hard, black, tight fitting box-like hat with a black tassel on the top, was worn making us all look slightly ridiculous. I felt uneasy, like a person who had been asked to accept a part in a play with which he is totally unfamiliar. I was wearing a costume not of my own choosing. Now we were really separated from everything we had experienced heretofore. We had left the 'world' behind. The world was a contaminated place. Toxic. The church has always fallen to the temptation to define boundaries between itself and the world. An authoritarian Christianity made this almost inevitable. The Catholic Church has always had a linear way of thinking – everything is either black or white, wrong or right, good or bad, venial or mortal. There is no room for shades of grey! As with the drawing of any boundary, the rigid definition of those who remained outside was as important as the definition of those who were inside. Those outside the 'Pale', especially Protestants or the lapsed, were definitely not 'one of us'. Our ministry in the future would be to put the world right – right with God and right with the church. Canon Mitchell, the President of Maynooth, in a speech at the centenary celebrations of Clonliffe College in 1960, said:

> Now the Council of Trent prescribed that candidates for the priesthood should be trained in seminaries or colleges, specially set aside for that purpose, where they should be guarded with special care from the contagion of the world.

'Contagion' – the word appears to carry implications of a disease worse than AIDS or the Black Death. If we didn't take precautions (rather like safe sex) we were likely to be contaminated. One of the primary objectives of a seminary training is to isolate the potential candidate for the priesthood from the possibility of infection by 'the world'. Not only were we set apart, but now this place we had left was inhabited by those a little less than we were. Such thoughts of superiority are easily expunged.

The Spiritual Exercises of St Ignatius
For all seminarians of the Dublin Diocese, life in Clonliffe began with *The Spiritual Exercises of St Ignatius* or, as it is more popularly known, 'the Thirty Days Retreat'. The worldview of St Ignatius, the founder of the Jesuits, took its first shape during Ignatius' own experience of conversion in 1521, particularly from his reading of *The Life of Christ* by Ludolph of Saxony. It was added to by his spiritual experiences at Manresa in 1522. Ignatius was the son of a Basque nobleman of ancient family. As I mentioned before, as a young man Ignatius was wounded by the French at

LIGHT AND DARKNESS

the siege of Pamplona. It was during his convalescence that he experienced his deep conversion. He felt an urge to share the extraordinary graces he had received with others. This led him to write notes, which became the core of his worldview from which he gradually developed his *Spiritual Exercises*. One author has claimed that, 'their graded pressure is aimed at bringing the retreatant to a definite commitment.'[1] Ignatius also wrote that 'we should put away completely our own opinion and give our entire obedience to our holy Mother the hierarchical church, Christ our Lord's undoubted Spouse.' I assume that was the purpose of the *Exercises* for us.

Our retreat was directed by a Pickwickian character, Fr Hal King SJ. He was a small, elderly, slightly bent man, with a bald head. On his small, round button nose were perched wire spectacles. Hall shuffled around the college in his shabby soutane, wearing what I presumed was a pair of bedroom slippers. He was silent and remote. Our retreat was geared towards those who sincerely desired to discover how he/she can please and serve God best, and who for about thirty days can withdraw from ordinary occupations in order to make four or five contemplations a day, alone with God, in complete silence.

The real story was that much of the retreat terrified me. The first week was like taking a giant enema. Similar to purging the bowels before surgery, this period was designed to purify the soul, free it from all attachments, and let the retreatant know how insignificant he or she was in the sight of God. It paints the history of sin and its consequences and our part in it. My imagination was in overdrive. The fires of hell were graphic in my imagination. I could hear the weeping and gnashing of teeth. Scruples about the past bubbled to the surface of my mind. On a scale of one to ten, my fear of hell rose to a solid eight! The words of Dante in the *Divina Commedia* hardly do justice to the sermons on hell of Fr King:

> Through me is the way to a sorrowful city. Through me is the way to eternal suffering. To me is the way to join the lost people … Abandon all hope you who enter!

The second week talked of acquiring virtue. For me, the principle memory is of a meditation on the Two Standards: one of

Christ; the other of Satan. The choice was mine. There was a chilling irrevocableness about the decision we were asked to make. This was followed by the Three Classes of Persons – postponers, half-hearted, and wholeheartedly decisive. What category was I going to belong to? We were told all about the three ways of being humble. The third and fourth week moved into what is called, in mystical language, the unitive or perfective way. This period was designed to establish habitual and intimate union with God.

This was a rugged exercise for teenagers – for that is what we were. Somehow, I became disengaged from the main body of my colleagues and adhered to the silence rigidly. It was only afterwards I learned that most of my colleagues had a relatively good time secretly relaxing in the Archbishop's garden when not attending the talks. They emerged from the experience marginally saner than I was! We were too immature for the experience and it didn't stick. I believe among a more mature group, more schooled in the language of spirituality, and advanced somewhat in the spiritual life, the *Spiritual Exercises* could have made a real difference. This is not to say that the exercise was a futile one. It introduced us, at the very least, to a world with which we were utterly unfamiliar.

Rugged Individualism Encouraged
Our training was designed to develop a rugged individualism capable of withstanding any pressures, particularly the isolation and loneliness of living alone. It was monastic in style. The diocesan priest was to be the archetypal Alexander Selkirk (on whom *Robinson Crusoe* was based), needing little companionship except that of God. Particular friendships were discouraged. A student could not enter the room of another student. To do so would be to risk expulsion. On our way to the university, our travelling companion was changed at regular intervals. There was camaraderie of sorts, but it seldom had the intimacy that allowed deep sharing of personal issues. There was a significant amount of silence throughout the day, in particular at night, when the 'solemn silence' reigned.

The unspoken premise to being a successful seminarian was, 'If you beat the system, we will ordain you.' The system included exaggerated deference to superiors, prolonged periods of silence, not forming 'particular friendships,' spiritual reading at mealtimes, wearing long soutanes and birettas, having your mail available for inspection, no newspapers or radio, and obeying the rule in a multiplicity of manifestations. It was a spiritual commando-type obstacle course. The recruit could be tested and assessed under pressure. With all the elan of a circus tightrope walker, a book on the Seminary Rule, first published in 1953, posed this conundrum: 'Does the rule bind me under pain of sin? If so, how serious a sin? If not, why not? Is there a difference between rules? And if there is no sin involved, what particular reason is there for keeping the rule?' Sin – if there was ever a word charged with dread, it was sin. So this was the nit-picking world where young men were formed, in isolation, for their greater task of saving the world.

Being called to the Dean's office was a bit like going to the dentist. He was a tall wispy, sad looking man, with black rimmed spectacles perched half way down his nose. He seemed old to me but probably wasn't more than thirty. He spoke in a low-pitched nasal tone of voice. He invariably seemed apologetic about himself. It was his responsibility to ensure that the rigid discipline of the College was maintained. On one occasion an interview I had with him went like this:

> 'Mr (one was never addressed by one's Christian name) Tierney, in my opinion the amount of newspaper cuttings you have received from home constitute a newspaper!' Silence. 'Have you anything to say?' Pregnant pause. 'Well, they are just about Saturday's rugby international,' I responded sheepishly, wondering why such a trivial issue was being made a fuss of. 'Well, I cannot let you have them,' said the Dean plaintively. He looked pained and upset as if he was being more deprived than I was. End of interview.

On another occasion I stood, like a POW at Colditz, as the Dean interrogated me on the possibility of my having contraband confectionery squirreled away somewhere. Among the student body were artful dodgers. They had developed secret trails that ensured that forbidden fruits arrived periodically. Caches of forbidden food – sweets, biscuits and cake – were hidden away. At times the caches were raided by uninvited students, to the consternation of the owner. He then agonised over the possibility that the Dean had discovered the 'goodies'. Swift retribution was awaited with dread. A visit to the dentist was similar to a pilot filing a flight plan. ETA, (estimated time of arrival) and the intended route had to be given. Deviations from the route were forbidden. Little had changed since the early days of the College. In his history of Clonliffe College, Dr Richard Sherry, quotes a seminarian of 1910:

> Our dean was Fr Matthew McMahon ... even in a seminary deans are a race apart and remain an enigma for the students. We always felt that we were 'agin' the dean, and he 'agin' us. 'Matt' – we were merciless in shortening names – was no exception. When he caught us out, we thought, in our boyish ways that it was rather like the queen's treatment for delinquents in 'Alice in Wonderland' – 'off with his head – execution first! – trial (there was seldom any) later.

I think Longfellow's *Tales of a Wayside Inn* best sums up the relationship between the staff (all priests) and the seminarians.

> Ships that pass in the night, and speak each other in passing:
> Only a signal shown and a distant voice in the darkness;
> So on the ocean of life we pass and speak to one another,
> Only a look and a voice; then darkness again and silence.

It appeared that the clerical staff were either ordered, or instructed, only to speak to the students, 'in so far as charity demanded'. There was none of the casual fraternisation between staff and students that I experienced in boarding school. In school it was considered quite ordinary for the staff to tog out and play football with us. They were always available to help with a debate speech, a family problem, or even engage in frivolous banter. No so in the seminary.

Most of the communication came to us students through student prefects, of whom I was one for a very brief period. The prefect was the eyes and ears of the disciplinary wing of the college. A prefect was assigned a section of the student body and he was in direct contact with their needs. He was also expected to report on their general behaviour.

On one occasion Canon Cathal McCarthy, the President of the College, very kindly drove me to my family home when I suffered a severe attack of asthma. He was an enigmatic figure. His presence brooded over the student body. Surprise and fear were his chief weapons. He was small and fat with innumerable chins. A leg amputation, as a consequence of a car accident, meant that the tap, tap, of his stick on the ground was enough to make us scatter. Serving the Canon's Mass, which we did in turn, gave rise to a trembling sweat and a sleepless night. I always felt he was a kindly man who feigned a mask of foreboding authority, as he felt his role demanded.

The College regime left comparatively few things to one's own free decision. The regulations took precedence, even over applying the counsels of mystical writers. The principle governing behaviour was implicit. It suggested that one should prefer that which gave less pleasure to that which gave more. Culturally, the seminary was a desert. Music and art were not fostered. We staged a play once a year and that was good fun. I still recall playing, Herr Tausch, in Denis Johnson's *The Moon on the Yellow River*. The library was exclusively stocked with books on spirituality, philosophy and theology. All this, at a stage of life when our contemporaries in the 'world' were getting married, bearing arms, starting families. Growing up to accept personal responsibility for one's actions was not part of the developmental curriculum of the seminary of the 50s and 60s. All decisions were made for us and were embedded in the rule. I still experience priests, well into their fifties and sixties, acting out the obsequiousness of seminary posturing. Many adopt a stance towards the bishop that they used when in the presence of the Dean or President of the seminary generations before. Some priests never developed a mature, manly independence, and are always waiting for the next directive from the bishop before they are willing to move.

CHAPTER FIVE

Learning Philosophy and Theology

All seminarians for our diocese went to University College Dublin. There we studied philosophy: Kant, Hume Lock, Descartes and, of course, Aquinas, who stretched the intellect. We read epistemology – 'How do we know that we know?' Metaphysics, the science of being. Logic was the road to certainty, which underpinned the whole stance of the church to the world. We had truth. That truth was arrived at by revelation (scripture and tradition) and by a system of deductive reasoning called logic. One of Aristotle's many contributions to the definition of certainty was the introduction of the syllogism, a means by which the validity of an argument could be assessed. So, all men are mortal, Socrates is a man ... therefore! Both premises seem fully tenable. No one has come up with an example of a man who has not died; it is part of the condition of being human. From these assumptions we drew the conclusion: 'Therefore Socrates is mortal.' Psychology, the philosophy of mind and organic matter, including the fundamentals of human adjustment, was an interesting part of the course. Cosmology – the metaphysics of space, time, motion and the methodology of physics and chemistry. We also learned of the proofs of the existence of God, taught to us by Professor John Horgan, an anodyne if remote figure, and a senior cleric of the Dublin diocese. Unlike every other faculty in the College, all our lecturers were clerics. All were strict Thomists, followers of the philosophy of the Dominican, St Thomas Aquinas, who lived in the thirteenth century. We were supposed to be learning Aristotelian philosophy *'ad mentem Sancti Thomae'*, (according to the mind of St Thomas), but we never opened a book of St Thomas. I appreciated philosophy; it cultivated an inquisitiveness of mind, something I never lost. It was a good preparation for four years of theology, which followed.

At the University we were forbidden to speak to lay students, 'except in so far as charity demanded.' Here we were,

LEARNING PHILOSOPHY AND THEOLOGY

neophytes, already isolated by our black suits and black homburg hats and by our preferential treatment in the canteen, and mute to boot! *Incongruous* seems inadequate to describe our predicament.

Theology also had its parts. Dogmatic theology presented the teachings of the church and the 'flimsy' arguments put forward by non-Catholics thinkers against our position. The latter were demolished as unworthy of too much consideration. Scripture could have been wonderful. However, we could do little more than study a bare outline of the Bible. Again, demolishing the scriptural interpretations presented by the 'rationalists,' bogey men who got a hard time, was important. Moral theology pecked incessantly at the notion of sin. Other courses, like pastoral theology, were interesting. Canon law, of course, was very important and we learned sections of it by heart, especially those parts that dealt with marriage. Once a week we had a talk from the Spiritual Director, who was a Vincentian.

At the end of the year, substantial money prizes were awarded to the outstanding students. I always thought it was peculiar to give money to seminarians for anything, but particularly for succeeding in exams. Some of the examinations were oral and in Latin. As our textbooks were mostly in Latin, it wasn't unduly burdensome to garner enough Latin to make an intelligent shot at answering the questions. We had a weekly oral Greek class, which entailed an examination.

Learning to preach
Homiletics was taught most intelligently. Fr Brian Connolly, our teacher, was a wonderfully creative man. He was a moderately tall man with black hair, black horn rimmed spectacles and a dark complexion. He wore a studious demeanour. Like the President, he too had a 'gammy' leg, and walked with a painful limp. He was a pious man, who spent a lot of time praying. At our very first meeting, we were asked to draw up an imaginary profile of a potential parishioner at a typical Sunday Mass. In those days, most Masses had packed congregations. This wasn't a cursory exercise. We had to get into the skin of another person. Name, age, job, magazines he or she read, what they did last night, how many brothers and sisters, transport to work, leisure

activities, level of education, eating habits, romantic attachments, holidays, wages, and on and on it went. Each of us carried that imaginary profile with us for the last four years in the seminary. Every so often, when we were at preaching practice, we would be stopped abruptly. 'What is your name? What time did you go to bed at last night? What magazines did you read this week?' And then the punch line – 'Do you think that Mary Magill, who was dancing up until three o'clock this morning, would have the foggiest idea of that you are trying to say?' Today, priests still use words like sanctification, salvation, sanctifying grace, redemption, paschal mystery, liturgy, even mortal sin – seldom pausing to think that such words are no longer among the lexicon of popular usage. One might as well be speaking Swahili in Red Square. In a recent study by Jesuit sociologist, Fr David Tuohy, one of his significant findings was that the young people in Ireland today, 'have lost the language and vocabulary of faith.' I can still hear the echo of Fr Connolly's voice when tempted to use a word no longer part of the vernacular.

On other occasions each of us was given an object, from a tractor to a biro, and told: 'Now I want you to sell that to the rest of the class. They must want passionately what you have to sell by the time you are finished.' So we sold bread, cars, pencils, hats, shoes, footballs or motor cars to one another. He was aware that the gospel, despite its unique claims, had to be sold like everything else. He was right. Finally, one might well be asked to mount the fifteen-foot steps of the ladder in the library. 'Now', he would say, 'you are Daniel O'Connell addressing a mass meeting before the age of microphones. I want you to lift your voice so that you will be heard down in O'Connell St.' The real test came in our final year. Each of the final year students in turn preached to their peers in the Oratory after night prayer. For some that was a nerve racking experience. I know that people continually complain about the quality of preaching in our churches. In defence, I would answer that, having listened to talks in golf club, at book launches, and retirement presentations over a lifetime, some by eminent celebrities, I think we are not as bad as we are made out to be.

Forty years after the events described above, I received a letter from a parishioner containing a lot of common sense wisdom. 'Is there anything more boring than the preacher who likes the sound of his own voice or the preacher who simply repeats in his own words, the readings to which we have just listened? Short, pithy observations and interpretations can add a spiritual dimension to the Mass. Anything else is a distraction and diverts our attention from what is being celebrated.'

Pastoral work
A welcome relief to the drudgery of College life was the weekly visit to the local Christian Brothers Schools at O'Connells, or St Laurence O'Toole's in Sherrif Street. This was our practical introduction to pastoral work. It was meant to supplement the more academic formation in the classroom, given by Fr Ó Cuív, an external teacher, then a curate in Blackrock. I was assigned to Laurence O'Toole's, known colloquially as 'Larryers'. My experience dealing with nine and ten year olds from the inner city was like a scene from an O'Casey play or the film *The Commitments*. Chaotic! Shambolic! I taught nothing. The struggle to keep order was time consuming. What did I learn? Whatever else you do in life, teaching is one vocation to be avoided! I have a huge admiration for teachers. Today, forty years later, I have an opportunity to observe at first hand the dedication, skill and patience of teachers. Most are wonderful people.

The paucity of our pastoral training was frightening. We were like amateur electricians being sent out, without ever having being taught how to use a circuit tester or a screwdriver.

Apart from our visits to the schools, I have no recollection of any other type of pastoral experience being offered through my seminary years. As a lay student at UCD, I chanced upon a poster in the Great Hall in Earlsfort Terrace (now the National Concert Hall) which read: *Legion of Mary, Introductory meeting. All Welcome. Refreshments afterwards.* I am sure the 'refreshment afterwards' was what appealed to me because, improbably as it may seem, I had never heard of the Legion of Mary. At that meeting a medical student from East Africa, Frank Quadros, gave a personal testimony of his faith that startled me. He was so enthusiastic, so zealous and passionate about his faith that I was impressed enough to join the Legion that night. At that time there were six or seven *praesidia* (groups) of the Legion in the University. Here were bright, creative, ambitious young men and women willing to risk embarrassment in their desire to witness to the gospel. I felt I was sharing in the experience of the early church. Since then, in 1958, I have always had an admiration for the Legion of Mary.

I organised a group of seminarians to accompany me on the *Peregrination Pro Christo* (Travel for Christ) on three or four occasions. Our Legion teams were mixed men and women, lay and clerical. This was my first regular contact with women, on a daily basis, since entering the seminary. Our services were offered to parishes in Birmingham, London, and Boston in the US. The work was usually house visitation. We either conducted a census of parishioners, or encouraged them to attend a parish retreat or mission. Well before Ireland experienced the winds of secularism, we were working in a post-Christian environment. We knocked on doors like clean-cut Jehovah Witnesses. It was a chastening experience to have to articulate one's faith and, on occasions, defend it robustly. It was an eye-opener. Traipsing up the stairs of high-rise public authority housing, only to have door after door closed in one's face, didn't necessarily lead to disappointment or discouragement. The minor successes were enough to build our faith to continue. In any walk of life if you believe in the product, no amount of difficulty is likely to intimidate. Douglas Hyde in his book *Dedication and Leadership* tells of leaving the Catholic Church in disillusionment. In the church he said that 'he had never been asked to do more that move the chairs in the village hall for "Father".' His first assignment as a Communist was to sell their daily newspaper *The Daily Worker* on the street corners of Liverpool as the bombs rained down, at the time before Russia had entered the war on the side of the Allies. He received abuse and derision. It didn't deflect him. He later returned to the church and became a public speaker in demand worldwide. Catholics seldom witness to their faith with evangelical passion.

We never had the verve of a William Booth, founder of the Salvation Army, who relished the bottles and the half bricks which rained down on every open-air meeting. A description of one meeting in Whitechapel in the East End of London claimed 'that while Brother Rose was speaking, about one hundred Irish fell upon him. One young man, very well dressed, seized him by the throat, another struck him a heavy blow to the cheek.'

I can recall on one occasion, in Boston, coming across an elderly man who was imprisoned by his sons. They were living off his welfare cheque. He was filthy. A gaping, festering wound in his neck limited his ability to speak to us. He lay on a filthy mattress. Beside him sat an aluminium bowl with a few mouldy potatoes. He looked like an Auschwitz survivor. A Puerto-Rican girl called Martha, from the local Legion of Mary, attended to his needs with tremendous compassion. I learned a lot about love from watching her goodness. On the streets of Soho in London, we did 'street contact'. This involved politely stopping people and asking for a moment to speak to them about the Catholic Church. What surprised me was the number of people who were willing to stop and talk. For the first time in my life I met people who had no faith or religion. The whole notion of belief in a supernatural life was inexplicable to them. We met prostitutes and strippers and barrow boys and Fagin-type characters. It was a wonderful on-the-hoof education.

During my time in the seminary I cannot recall any colleague expressing doubts about issues of faith or morals. There appeared to be, at least outwardly, a complete unanimity of faith among the students. If there were difficulties, they rarely surfaced, either in class or in casual conversation.

Celibacy
Surprisingly, celibacy was seldom a topic of chat or debate among seminarians. It was there like a suspected ghost that one couldn't admit caused inner fear and apprehension. It was a proverbial elephant in the kitchen that no one mentioned. In six years in Clonliffe, I can only recall two talks on celibacy. Apart from the sentence, 'even an elephant sleeps after intercourse', the content of each has deserted my memory completely. I know for a fact that many of us student clerics developed an obsessive fear of sexuality. Sex was like a nuclear cauldron, within which lay explosive possibilities for sinning, thereby making us unsuitable to be priests. Bad thoughts, masturbation, forbidden fantasies, burrowed into the mind. On one occasion, I now em-

barrassingly recall tearing pages from a book lest they continue to fuel fantasies of forbidden pleasures. Weekly confession was always a painful experience. Its healing effects were never more than transitory. A popular book of the 1950s fairly starkly summed up the choice:

> For the aim – and this we must admit if we are honest – is the attainment of a summit, towards which there leads a path of agonising loneliness. To renounce the natural desire for happiness and human affection in order to be bound to God alone, to be willingly made prisoner and flooded by his love, so that, being thus transformed, one may for God's sake love men and serve them – this is something that goes beyond nature. It implies a process of continual death and rebirth which exacts a difficult and often bloody price.

It would be interesting to have a psychologist and a mystical theologian interpret the underlying strains of thoughts in this passage.

We were encouraged to keep 'custody of the eyes.' This meant glancing demurely at the ground at the passing of a pretty girl. On one occasion, the archbishop advised me if I ever found myself alone in a room with a woman to make sure the door remained opened. I was puzzled. Was it that women were a source of temptation and to be kept strictly at arms length? We were hardly aware that the type of stress involved in the acceptance of a life of celibacy looks quite different from within the walls of a community of congenial fellow-celibates, and from the point of view of a solitary bachelor in a parish of families. A cold shower was never enough to reconcile the differences!

CHAPTER SIX

Seminary Spirituality

We followed the perfection model of spirituality, based on the scripture, 'Be perfect as your Heavenly Father is perfect.' An impossibility! Only God is perfect, and the good news is that God loves imperfect beings. The spirituality of perfection is demoralising because it is self-defeating. It produced a lot of sadness, self-criticism and, ultimately, capitulation. It was a joyless, inquisitorial, type of spirituality. I have a hunch that a lot of priests live out unhappy lives, fretting at the impossible goals set for them by their seminary training. Has this anything to do with the fact that so many priests and religious, who were formed in this model of spirituality, finally gave up the struggle?

We meticulously filled in a monthly *ratio mentis*, a chart; today it might be called a spreadsheet, although it looked more like a bingo card. It detailed every aspect of our daily examination of conscience, spiritual reading, weekly confession, study. Each month, the Spiritual Director, a Vincentian Father, received our chart for inspection. It wasn't unlike a chart used by those practising the Ovulation Method of contraception! It usually formed the basis for any further discussion. It was a graph of spiritual progress. I was doubtful then, and I am even more so now, that such a regime had anything to contribute to growth, spiritual or personal.

Our spirituality was formed by the *Imitation of Christ*, which was read to us, chapter by chapter, at mealtime each day. In the time set aside for spiritual reading, we were recommended: St Francis de Sales' *Introduction to the Devout Life* (St Francis de Sales was writing for noblemen and women in the courtly world of seventeenth century Savoy); Abbot Marmion's *Christ in his Mysteries*; and Fourard's *Life of Christ* and St John of the Cross.

The message of St John of the Cross was a severe one. The very first steps on the spiritual life were laid out by St John in the following precepts:

Strive always to prefer, not that which is easiest, but that which is most difficult;
Not that which is most delectable, but that which is most unpleasing;
Not that which gives most pleasure, but rather that which gives least;
Not that which is restful, but that which is wearisome.

A lot of what we read and heard led me at least into a valley of introspection: inquisitive whether one was measuring up to the sort of spiritual progress mentioned by the mystical writers. An empty place in the pew at Morning Prayer usually meant that a companion had chosen *vota secularia* – to leave. One or two leaving in a week sent morale crashing. I am sure it gave rise to a lot questioning, 'What am I doing here when those better than me are leaving?'

I wasn't aware of what seems so blindingly obvious now, namely, the mismatch between the training for the priesthood provided by the seminary, and the actual life I would encounter in a few short years. It is natural for people to comment that we had seven years to test our vocation, but that isn't really true. At least I now fail to see any but the most tenuous relationship between what happened in the seminary and the life I experienced as a priest. In the seminary we lived in a companionable community, by now culturally conditioned to behave as one. Later we would live in isolation, our behaviour dictated only by willpower, grace and the demands of parishioners.

Undoubtedly, the emphasis has shifted since the 60s. The Apostolic Exhortation of Pope John Paul II, *Pastores Dabo Vobis*, on the formation of priests, speaks of Jesus in terms of friendship and recognises the great spiritual value of searching for Jesus. The Pope also writes of the necessity of pastoral formation, including pastoral and charitable dimensions.

In those days, there was no question of working at a secular job during our long holidays. There were times when some of us, at least, sat around playing cards and backing horses or playing golf. Golf and petrol were cheap then, and some clubs were generous enough to give a reduction to clerics. I made the acquaintance of golf clubs like Greystones, Delgany, the Curragh,

Carlow, the Castle, Baltray, Mullingar, Elm Park and Edmondstown. We had a floating four ball that included Peter Kilroy, Brian Harkins (RIP), Paddy Ryan, Eamonn Cotter and others. The thick gorse of Greystones, and the sheep on the Curragh, often frustrated our attempts to be anything more than plumbers. Brian's passion for horses was like Billy Bunter's for tuck. He couldn't keep away from them. At times we sat in front of a grainy black and white television while he explained the intricacies of betting to us. 'Two to one the field,' never meant much to me. Poker was our chosen game. The cut and thrust of the game was, at times, as tense as a penalty shoot-out in a World Cup game. The stakes were modest but that didn't dampen the ardour.

A career and a marriage
On one occasion I approached the Spiritual Director to discuss the authenticity of my vocation. Did God, in fact, call me? How was I to know? One booked a spot with the Spiritual Director by leaving one's biretta outside his door during study time. The owner of the biretta ahead of yours then called you. When I walked into the room, the Director, a tall man with owlish features and a perfectly bald head, glanced up from a radio he was repairing. 'Well?' he said questioningly. Before I sat down, I knew he expected me to explain my business. 'Father, I was wondering if I should leave the seminary. I am not sure if I have a vocation,' I stammered. 'Don't be silly, boy,' he said firmly – still tinkering with the radio with his screwdriver. I was at a loss to pursue the conversation and with a mumbled excuse I left his room.

I had a foreboding about the life I was about to embark on. There were moments of real indecision, kept mostly to myself. I think I eventually fell into an 'It will be all right on the night' attitude, and steadfastly refused to think about issues of vocation any more. I believe the official attitude was that a vocation (call) was authenticated by the very fact that your character proved worthy in the eyes of the staff, and that the bishop agreed to ordain you. The 'call' was from the ordaining bishop. We understood that a vocation was not a special revelation, a visitation or an inner voice from God.

Choosing a way of life in the secular world makes allowances for mistakes. People change from one career choice to another. With a seminarian it is different. You are doing more than choosing a career. You are choosing a career and a marriage. 'You are a priest for ever according to the order of Melchideck.' Like baptism and confirmation, the sacrament of priesthood left, 'an indelible mark that couldn't be erased'. One was choosing a way of life and a wife – you became married to the Holy Roman Catholic Church forever. A ghastly mistake would carry dire and life-long consequences, too horrible to contemplate. The life-long disgrace to one's family was always uppermost in one's mind. We didn't have female friends. The likelihood of our vocation being tested was improbable.

Seminaries are spartan institutions. I can recall sitting with my feet in a basin of hot water to keep my feet warm in the bitter winter cold. Another device used by students was a large mineral bottle of hot water in the bed as a DIY hot jar. In our early years, without running water in the rooms, we 'slopped out' just as our near neighbours did in Mountjoy Prison. A rugged masculinity hung in the air. No flowers or pot-pourri, the familiar sign of a feminine presence, to relieve the tang of carbolic soap. This was Mount Athos without the Greek weather.

In Clonliffe College there was an annual cull, not unlike the 'glorious twelfth' in Scotland, when the grouse season opens. Coming towards the summer holiday, an ominous sight was the head prefect prowling the corridors with a list in his hand. A call to the President was filled with foreboding for the victim. It usually meant that the student was told, ever so kindly, that 'he wasn't suitable for the Dublin Diocese.' If the student was from the country, the reason for 'expulsion' could be as trivial as an unsuitable accent. Many who were 'let go' made good in other dioceses – indeed, in some instances, they became bishops. Everyone was expendable, as there was always someone waiting to take our place.

Visits from parents were allowed once a month. They took place in a large hall. The ambiance never lent itself to anything but peripheral chatter. Visits for me were an embarrassment. To conjure up an interesting conversation from the trivia of the lives we led would have required lateral thinking on a high plain.

The seminary was full of highly motivated, idealistic young men. The surprise is that, nearly forty years later, the vast majority of them have retained their idealism. Many no longer see the church as the pristine light shining in the darkness. Nevertheless, their commitment to the people of God is undiminished. They are still generous, prayerful and, for the most part, intelligent people. Had they not decided to be priests, many would have ended up in the judiciary, the teaching profession, or as professional carers or, indeed, politics. There are very few truly cynical priests. I try, on occasions, to stand aside, and look at my companions on the journey. By and large, they are good men, still striving to serve as best they can. I have conducted a lot of retreats for priests. More often than not I come away humbled by the generous lives many of them lead. Now they, like me, are devastated, by recent happenings.

When I walk through the gradually decaying building of Clonliffe now, no warm emotions of nostalgia arise within me. It is like gazing at the corpse of an unknown person. Within, I experience icy cold neutrality. No regrets, no bitterness, no anger – nothing. There is baffling amnesia of much of my time there, almost as if all this never happened. There are no places within the huge campus that I would like to revisit. When I revisit Clongowes, I search out, within the changed contours of the place, spots where significant things happened – even if it was only playing 'push-penny.' The pew in the College chapel where I sat or knelt day after day is still special fifty years later. I look, with a mixture of gratitude and fear, at the Confessional where Fr 'The Dog' McGlade SJ ministered to us youngsters. He was never inquisitive, and always gave the same penance – three Our Fathers and three Hail Marys. But, with Clonliffe – nothing.

There is a growing demand for a return to the type of seminary training I received. Some think the discipline, orthodox teaching and rigid supervision is still the best way to train young men for the priesthood. I disagree. Superficially, like a derelict building recently whitewashed, it might look good, but it does not contribute to personal growth and maturity. A recent attempt to turn the clock back, initiated by a reactionary ‚conservative Austrian Bishop, Klaus Krenn, went horribly wrong.

Revelations of an unsavoury sex scandal in the seminary, run very much on traditional lines, made headlines across the world. The scandal involving staff and students included the downloading of child pornography and of homoerotic behaviour. A healthier model of spirituality is one in which life is seen as a journey, a pilgrimage. It is a model guided not so much by the voice of authority, or a bell, or fear of penalty, but by a sense of personal responsibility. A developmental type of spirituality is built on a personal response to God's call rather than obedience to a set of rules or Canon Law. This spirituality admits, rather acknowledges, that we are flawed beings. We are a mixture of sin and virtue, good and evil, light and darkness. That's okay with God. I can recall the enormous burden that was lifted from my shoulders when I finally accepted that God loved me as I was. He loved me when I was good but even more so when I wasn't!

It was at the Sangre de Christo Retreat Centre, in Sante Fe, New Mexico that thirty years later, in 1994, that I was able, for the first time, to offer to God the whole of me – the good and the bad, the light and the darkness. It's never easy to be honest, especially with oneself. One of the most common mistakes we all make, but especially we priests, is to believe that we have successfully got rid of all that primitive savagery within. Those of us who grew up in a restrictive atmosphere – one that was narrow, demanding, closed, legalistic, tense, and rigid, have a great many things to deny and repress. There were so many thoughts that we were not allowed to have, so many words that we were not allowed to speak, so many behaviours they we were not allowed to perform. Necessity demanded that these be repressed. We had to present to the word the face that was expected of us – the face that wins rewards and praise; the face surrounded with an aura of piety. We were so good at maintaining the façade of goodness and piety that the Eamon Casey incident, and the subsequent sex abuse scandals, sent the church in Ireland into freefall. People were genuinely shocked to the core.

Around this time I can remember reading a book which deeply affected me, *Making Friends with Your Shadow – How to accept and Use Positively the Negative Side of Your Personality*. Millar writes about facing your shadow, your true self, as equivalent to 'drinking your own spittle'. I think reading that book was a moment of truth for me. The moment of truth is a turning point on our journey. It comes when the full weight of our inability to handle our lives with fruitfulness finally breaks through, and we admit it. In the moment of truth, we stop denying or trying to flee from the brokenness of our own world. We admit the painful truth of it. With that, we take our personal stand in the truth. For an alcoholic it might be the time when his or her youngest child shouts out in anger and frustration: 'Daddy, I hate you! You're nothing but a drunk!' The moment of truth might come for a married couple when they realise, with dismay, that what they are now is not a married couple, but married singles. They stop in horror at the crossroads and the moment of truth. The moment of truth might come for a workaholic when his tearful wife says in sadness and pain, 'I'm so lonely.' The moment of truth can be a turning point. I know it was for me in 1994. I now know that the moment of truth is a painful blessing that God wants all of to have. I can at last stop pretending I am good. When I came to terms with my own imperfections, sinfulness if you like, there was less need to relate to the world through a mask of respectability. Kurtz and Ketcham, in *The Spirituality of Imperfection*, put it like this:

> For to be human is, after all, to be other than 'God' and so it is only in the embracing of our torn self, only in the acceptance that there is nothing 'wrong' with feeling 'torn' that one can hope for whatever healing is available and can thus become as 'whole' as possible. Only those who know darkness can truly appreciate light; only those who acknowledge darkness can even see the light.

I am struggling, like everyone else. Now I can live in freedom without covering up any more. This style of spirituality would be too uncertain for those who wish to return to the rigorous monastic spirituality of the seminary of the sixties. The desire to get back to a spirituality that can be measured, is very much in tune with the rise of fundamentalism in many religions throughout the world. The need for certainty appeals to a particular type of personality. To be honest, we left Clonliffe and went into the world as spiritual pygmies. Is it any wonder that so many priests abandoned the active ministry? We, recently ordained priests, were like the group of climbers that Jon Krakauer tried to take on a guided ascent to the summit of Everest in 1996. Four perished. The relatively inexperienced climbers were no match for the mountain. Each of them had paid as much as €65,000 to be taken safely up Everest – into an apparent death trap. The seminary training we received and the reality we faced were like Jon Krakauer's group – fumbling and hesitant. We were waiting for the mountain to gobble us up. The reality was harsher than the starry-eyed vision we had lived on for so long.

PART TWO

On Being a Priest

CHAPTER SEVEN

Ordination

Ordination to the priesthood was preceded by a number of intermediate steps. Nowadays, clerics (in effect laymen) glory in wearing traditional clerical garb. In fact, we were lay men in the seminary for the first five years. It was the conferring of tonsure that marked the movement from the lay to the clerical state. The bishop cut a tiny bit of hair from the back of the head. The hair quickly grew back again and that was the end of that! I was now a cleric of the Holy Roman Catholic Church. Then there were Minor Orders like lector, porter, exorcist and acolyte. These were administered by the bishop, but were quite meaningless. We couldn't cast out devils, nor were we given the keys of the College or the tabernacle. Yet to be denied these Orders, even temporarily, was a severe warning shot across the bows from the College authorities. 'Watch your step,' was the message. It was the equivalent of a rugby player being sent to the 'sin bin' nowadays. To have one's Orders postponed was to be a marked man. Sub-Diaconate was the Major Order that truly marked a Rubicon in the journey towards priesthood. We wore the full clerical black suit, roman collar and, of course, hat outdoors. The sub-deacon could assist, fully vested, at a High Mass. This had its own particular kudos within the narrow confines of the seminary.

We began to recite the Divine Office daily – in Latin. The Office consisted of eight canonical hours – Matins, Lauds, Prime, Sext, None, Vespers and Compline. The recitation of the Office took about an hour. Each word, was said, that is 'articulated', with the lips. It had to be finished within the twenty-four hour period under pain of sin! To complete your Office under the glare of the headlight of your car was kosher, to wait until you returned home to complete it in relative comfort, after midnight, was not. Matins particularly was a long haul. The readings from scripture and commentaries from the Fathers of the Church were invariably incomprehensible to me. It was like reading a blockbuster novel, that is enjoyable in a way, but one keeps wondering will the end ever come. The final major step was the conferring of the Diaconate. Now we could distribute Holy Communion to the laity. It also signalled an end to serious study.

We began to learn how to say Mass, in Latin. Each of the deacons had a tiny altar erected in his room for daily practice. Every gesture of the body, hands, and lips was regulated by specific rules called rubrics. The *Roman Missal* spelled out in black the words the priest must say and in red the actions he must perform. Footnotes in the manual regularly discussed whether the breech of a particular rubric was a venial or mortal sin. The tone of voice, whether the priest's head was to be bowed slightly or profoundly; whether the head as well as the body should be bowed; whether the hands were to be open or shut; how, if open, the hands should be strictly parallel to each other, with the tips of the fingers at the width and level of the shoulder, were all strictly regulated. '*Dominus Vobiscum*' we said, opening the hands and arms shoulder width and no more. Many of the prayers were learnt by heart. Each week we had a formal lesson on saying Mass. All this was more nerve racking than a driving test. At our first Mass, a senior priest stood at our shoulders, to ensure that no serious mistakes were committed.

Then there were invitations to be sent out to family, relatives and friends. Cards were printed with pious prayers for distribution to well-wishers. Suits, soutanes and vestments had to be bought – a bride's trousseau paled in comparison. I still use a beautiful chalice my parents gave me, on ordination, forty years on.

In those days, an ordination and First Mass was not unlike a wedding. The preparations were as meticulously made, and the expense was just as considerable. It was usual to have an elaborate meal in a hotel after the First Mass. My ordination breakfast (as it was called) was held in the old Jury's Hotel in Dame St, long since gone. Under the personal attention of the manager, the late Johnny Opperman, nothing was spared. There were speeches and toasts, and must else besides, apart from the inevitable disco! The priest donned an invisible aura of pure light. He was feted. He was now a Brahmin, a Mullah, and a Guru to

ORDINATION

his family and peers. Sydney Smith wrote in 1855, 'There are three sexes – men, women and clergymen.' Now I was to be the latter forever! There were three of us – Maurice O'Shea, Peter Kilroy and myself – from St Thérèse Parish, Mt Merrion, Dublin, ordained for the diocese on the same day. Our family and friends gave us generous gifts, many of which I still have.

I was ordained on 17 May 1964. This was the year Cassius Clay pulled off one of boxing's greatest surprises, by beating an apparently invincible Sonny Liston to take the heavyweight championship of the world. Beatle mania took off. Pope Paul visited the Holy Land, where he met Patriarch Athenogoras – a first meeting of religious leaders from East and West for 500 years.

I remember little about the ordination ceremony. Nineteen of us prostrated ourselves on the ground before Archbishop John Charles McQuaid. The words of the Litany of the Saints washed over us, invoking the intercession of those who had gone before us. The archbishop imposed hand on our heads individually. This is the sacramental transmission of orders. Many previously ordained priests and prelates followed, each imposing hands with pressure and solemnity. Then our hands were anointed with oil and bound in cloth, and touched to the chalice and paten, which would be our tools of the trade for evermore. My mother kept the cloth that bound my hands, right up to the time of her death. We promised obedience to the bishop and then he imposed hands again transferring to us the power to forgive sin.

On ordination day the priest gives his first blessing to family and friends and then proffers his hands to be kissed. These are holy hands. They are to be God's instruments in offering sacrifice, in forgiving sin, in anointing the sick, in baptising children. At the time I felt horribly ill at ease. I was no saint and didn't want to be treated differently. I found my change of status embarrassing. Suddenly I was holy, not by any inner change of heart, but by the rite of ordination. I realise, of course, that it wasn't necessarily the man who was being honoured, but the role. Even still I feel uncomfortable. There were expectations to be lived up to – mostly the expectations of the laity. Quite honestly, it scared me, and still does to this day. I didn't want to be different. Driving out to the ordination reception, I recall asking myself – what have I done? Is this what I wanted? I wanted the opportunity to prove myself like my lay peers had to do. I hardly got that chance. I didn't experience any spiritual euphoria as a consequence of ordination. My doubt was my possible inability to live up to such an exalted calling. I asked myself, over and over again, was I worthy to celebrate Mass, to minister the Body of Christ to others and to mediate his forgiveness and love? I felt like a lonely monk on Mount Athos, the place where no female, animal or human, has been permitted since the 11th century.

Our exclusion from many facets of life was hardly that extreme, but it was real. The teaching of St Ambrose in the 4th century had percolated deeply into the church's thinking. He wrote: 'Marriage is honourable but celibacy is more honourable; that which is good need not be avoided, but that which is better should be chosen.'

After ordination, the newly ordained was not his own man. At that time the Maynooth Statutes of 1956 strictly regulated every facet of priestly conduct. Any social contact with women, no matter how pious they were, was *'prorsus evitet'* (entirely to be avoided). It was forbidden to take any woman alone in one's car as a companion, and to disobey this rule was to incur the possibility of appropriate sanctions, not excluding suspension from the priesthood. We couldn't play violent games, like Gaelic football or hurling, play cards after midnight, attend the theatre, race meetings, leave the parish for a night, or incur debts of over £200, without permission. Even teetotallers were forbidden to enter *'tabernas'* (hotel or lounge bars,) and clerical dress was regulated in detail. Many hilarious classes were spent discussing whether one could stop playing cards at five to twelve and recommence at five minutes past midnight without breaking the Statutes. Did a priest break the Maynooth Statutes if he gave his mother a lift in his car? Or his housekeeper, if he had one? There were stories of priests reading the Breviary (Divine Office) by the headlights of their cars, standing on hillsides near local race courses and standing in the wings of the Abbey or Gaiety to see a play. Some priests even played on their County Gaelic team under assumed names. I recall, dimly, Archbishop McQuaid complaining about a Fr Gavin who played for the Irish Rugby team in the 1950s. I believe that he approached his bishop in

England to pressurise him to have Gavin removed from the team. Thankfully, he was rebuffed. In those days the Irish rugby team had their one and only practice in College Park in Trinity, on the Friday before an International. As a little school boy in short trousers, I scampered on to the field and managed to get Fr Gavin's autograph, little knowing that he was probably in the eye of a storm at the time. One can more easily appreciate the conundrum of how many angels can fit on the head of a pin, coming from those educated in the surreal environment we priests moved in.

Our training created a race apart. Our vocabulary and mindset changed. We hardly realised that in many ways we had become isolated. A chasm, eerie in its depth, was created between ourselves and the lay people we were to serve. No doubt the training for other professions, medicine, the law, the military, had defining features that set them apart. But, it was celibacy that was that was the irrevocable wedge that separated laity from clergy. It effectively excluded the priest from a whole range of experiences inherently natural and wholesome. We became part of an honourable and exclusive club. It wasn't long until we lost 'the lay mind'. Our language, vocabulary and thinking became essentially clerical. Even today, in the Funeral liturgy, we use phrases like, 'the supper of the Lamb'. Incomprehensible to an average parishioner!

Companionship was to be found among the clerical brethren. Too much fraternisation with the laity was subtly discouraged. With clerical companionship came loyalty to each other and the system. There was fun. Thank God for golf and football! There was friendship with those laity who could see beyond the collar to the person. Some of my happiest times were the card games I participated in with Dublin bus drivers and conductors after their evening shift in my first parish. I met, and grew to appreciate deeply, many of the wonderful working class people of Dublin through my involvement with the Community Games. This was a great tutoring experience at the very beginning of my priesthood.

We didn't see ourselves as functionaries but as men set aside to witness to the gospel in our actions and in our lives. Our desire was to serve after the manner of Jesus. This was the motivation of most of the priests I knew. In the early days, we researched and wrote learned papers on theological topics, which we delivered to each other. Most of us were 24 hours on duty. With the priest, his home and his office are one and the same. In the large conurbations of Dublin, the doctor, the teachers, the nurse, came from outside the area, but not the priest. In the beginning we lived in substandard accommodation. I lived in a dingy, tiny bed-sitter in the flatlands of Rathmines, for which I paid £2.10s a week. The room was so small the wardrobe was on the landing. We were not allowed a car at that time, so many priests, myself included, rode scooters, mopeds or motorbikes.

There were compensations. The privileged access into the lives of people was intuitively sacred. The priest was trusted and his advice often sought. A very special time was death. The death of a parishioner meant that the priest, and the bereaved, were up against the mystery of loneliness and were confronted with unanswerable questions. At times like these, if there weren't good priests they would have to be invented! I experienced a lot of job satisfaction. The support and camaraderie of people was wonderful. There were very long hours in the confessional. From the day of my ordination I felt uncomfortable with the detail people felt they needed to confess. I still do. On a recent retreat attended by many old people they were still worrying about sins committed before I was born. It just doesn't seem right. Yet, many people were comforted and did receive help. We all have a need to share the intimacies of our lives with a trusted companion. Nowadays the chat show has replaced the confessional. More about this later.

Hearing Confessions
Shortly after ordination, the Parish Priest of Mount Merrion, Dublin, asked me to hear Confessions in Linden Nursing Home. But, it was only later, when I was again given a temporary assignment to Glasnevin Parish, that I appreciated the awesomeness of this sacrament. I felt trusted by the people. I was humbled by their openness. I appreciated their sincerity. I couldn't believe that my advice would be that important to anyone. People wanted a priest who was compassionate and kind. But, despite the personality of the priest, it was forgiveness and heal-

ORDINATION

ing they wanted above all. On a number of occasions, I have experienced what I can only attribute to the spiritual gifts of knowledge and wisdom. There were times when I listened to myself giving advice. It was as if I was having an out-of-body experience. I was saying to myself, 'This advice I am giving is correct, but it is not you who is speaking.' I knew that the advice I was giving was beyond my personal competence and level of knowledge, and yet I was utterly convinced that what I was saying was sound. On a number of occasions, I was given an insight into the core of a person's condition and was able to help. These are not personal gifts but the gifts of the Holy Spirit.

The history of the sacrament of penance records a strong tradition of confession as healing and therapeutic. It places the priest in the role of 'physician of the soul'. He is the 'spiritual doctor to heal wounds of the spirit'. We believe that every sacrament is an 'act of Christ'. In the Sacrament of Reconciliation it is Christ who forgives. It is Christ who heals.

On two occasions I had unusual experiences in relation to this sacrament. On one occasion I was descending in a lift from the tenth floor of the then London Tara Hotel. A man entered the lift a few floors later. He gave me one look, and said immediately, 'Will you hear my confession?' He had the look of a man in pain. We hit the ground floor and ascended immediately to his room. We had a good talk, followed by absolution. He left a free man. On another occasion I was in a bank doing my normal business. Out of the corner of my eye I noticed a man looking at me. 'Do I know him?' I asked myself. As I walked to my car, the man caught up with me and made the same request – 'Will you hear my confession?' We got into my car and he unburdened himself and left with the healing and forgiveness of Christ.

Of course, we come to God through our wounds. Our very imperfections – what we call our sins, what therapy calls our 'sickness', what philosophy calls our 'errors' – are precisely what brings us closer to the reality that no matter how hard we try to deny it, we are not the ones in control here. And this realisation, inevitably and joyously, brings us closer to God. Proud people hardly need confession! In the words of Bill Wilson, a founder of Alcoholics Anonymous, 'It seems absolutely necessary for most of us to get over the idea that man is God.' I have always had an enormous respect for the work of Alcoholics Anonymous. They look to a 'higher power', knowing that their problem is greater than they themselves can handle. They confess with disarming frankness, and no little humility, and they take one day at a time.

As children, confession was like magic. A clean, fluffy white 'soul' emerged from the dark anonymity of the Confessional. We were walking on air. It wasn't long before the dark clouds of temptation and sin approached once more. We fell into the dark chasm. Back again, only to emerge fluffy white. Again and again, the cycle was repeated, to the point of desperation. Then the realisation dawned that this wasn't working. In frustration many people simply gave up going to confession. Anyway, the sky didn't fall in on them, nor did the world end, with their spiritual petulance. They could still be happy. Mortal sin, and the deterrence of eternal death and damnation, no longer worked. When fear fails what can replace it? Wiping the slate clean or scraping the barrel were terms used for confession. It was an action rather than a journey. As a priest once said to me 'What difference does moving a bit of air over a person's head make?'

A practical consequence of pluralism and of the psychologising of our culture, is that it has become fashionable to be non-judgemental, not only towards others, but also towards oneself. The pluralistic climate tends to encourage a perspective that all systems are equally valid. The unique claims of the Catholic Church tend to be dismissed as arrogance. Neutrality in all things religious is viewed as a virtuous thing. This is considered as the sign of a truly enlightened society. What is considered good for me, is good. What is bad for me is bad. Objective claims of absolute moral principles are resisted.

In a few short years we have witnessed the virtual demise of this sacrament. It is a rare week when a priest in a parish hears more than a dozen confessions. There is a growing reluctance to apply any external norms of behaviour to how one orders one's life. One hears the catch-cry, 'Nobody is going to tell me how to live my life.' The word freedom now means the ability to be a self-determining human being. The principle of life adopted by many is 'live and let live', with a tendency to resist or even deny external social restraints on our freedom. Many are determined

ORDINATION

to choose whatever lifestyle appeals to them. Even clearly enunciated scriptural principles are denied as a restraining force. The scriptures do present us with objective norms to follow in ordering our relationship with God, our neighbour and the world. The teachings of Jesus Christ are fundamentally ordered towards a life of love. The breaching of the demands of the 'law of love' is hardly seen any more as sin.

In recent years it has become quite common for a priest to be called after a person has died. It is rare for a priest to be called even in danger of death. I assume the attitude of 'God will understand' negates the need for any mediator on the road to reconciliation. There is hardly even a residual belief in the mediatorship of the church or its minister in the forgiveness of sin. That is, if sin is even recognised! Sin is a word that has slipped from the English lexicon. Those who are angry with the church have tended to view confession as an exercise of power. Even an abuse of power! Even those who frequent the sacrament have such an underdeveloped sense of conscience that they find it difficult to find sins worthy of confession!

CHAPTER EIGHT

Archbishop McQuaid

We were ruled over by the enigmatic Archbishop, John Charles McQuaid. He was a complex man. McQuaid was like the Holy Spirit, you never got to know him except through the effects of his actions. I sensed he even puzzled himself. He reigned like a mediaeval prince bishop. His house was situated in baronial splendour, in its own grounds, in Killiney, a posh suburb of Dublin. He commuted daily, by chauffeur-driven car, to the archiepiscopal palace in Drumcondra. His personal lifestyle was frugal. The opulence of his surroundings, I have no doubt, were due to the exaggerated view he held of the importance of his office. His retinue was there to serve him and, in doing so, was serving God and the Church. His successor, Archbishop Ryan, also felt there was a particular aura divinely attached to the office that made him different.

McQuaid managed to weave an air of mystery and mystique around his person that sent out the signal that here was somebody special. He had a rigidity of thought, rooted in a strictly hierarchical model of church, where at all times he was the prince/bishop. He was so politically adroit that he effectively influenced both church and state. Leadership in the church back then was seldom discussed. It was a leadership by dictate, by fear or by divine authority. The apparently frigid Pope Pius XII was so removed from the ordinary affairs of humanity that the nature of his leadership was accepted rather than questioned. He had such an ethereal quality about him, that it was difficult to think of him as really human. McQuaid was somehow in the same mode. He got things done, but 'big brother is watching you' was the only detectable inspiration behind the motivation for action.

As students, each of us, well over a hundred at the time, had an individual interview with Archbishop McQuaid. This interview lasted several hours with some students. It invariably included a dissertation on the 'facts of life', and included specific advice on personal hygiene. It made me squirm. Awe is the best word to describe how we priests viewed him. Not a hair, clerical or lay, moved in the diocese that he didn't know about. It is said that he used to drive around the city at night in a car with tinted windows to apprise himself of what was going on. I never felt relaxed in his presence. I was unnerved by his deep-set, wide, boring eyes, his mysteriously quizzical smile, and his interminable fingering of the pectoral cross that hung from his neck,

I was the Archbishop's trainbearer for a number of years. Part of my job was to help him vest before liturgical ceremonies, which included taking off his street shoes and putting on his, 'buskins and sandals'. These were purple socks and purple clog-like shoes, which he wore at ceremonies. The buskins were attached to his trousers with safety pins! He sat, while I knelt at his feet. Invariably, nothing passed between us. Then, like a pageboy at a royal ritual, I walked a few paces behind him, with head demurely bowed. The purple train, several feet long, was tucked between my arms. In later life, as his instigation, I got to know him better. On one occasion, he gave me a biography of J. Edgar Hoover to read. On the inside cover, the infamous chief of the FBI wrote flatteringly to the archbishop, in his own handwriting. Birds of a feather ...? Occasionally, he asked leading questions about personalities or events – no doubt to add to his vast data bank of information. He rarely responded to my opinions and, thereby, didn't reveal his own attitude or opinion.

I am an asthmatic. Archbishop McQuaid, the son of a doctor, took a particular interest in my condition. This included helping me with breathing exercises in his study in Drumcondra. On another occasion, when I was in London working with the Legion of Mary, he sent me money with a cryptic one-liner, 'To help you with your bus fares.' After his retirement, he invited me to his home in Killiney for afternoon tea. I was uneasy and embarrassed at these meetings. His gimlet eyes bored into my soul. The thought, 'What does he know about me?' surfaced instantly. Maybe I had a guilty conscience! The chemistry wasn't there to construct a friendship. Had he lived at the time of the Inquisition, he would have made a wonderful inquisitor. I had a sense that he was a lonely man who was searching for companionship or the affirmation of friends. Is it too farfetched to speculate that McQuaid used power and influence as a compensation for loneliness? He needed to matter to someone. To be important in the life of another matters to most people. McQuaid mattered. He ruled over a considerable empire – parishes, schools, hospitals, social works, but it was the power he wielded that mattered, rather than the man.

As a pastor he was visionary and farseeing. Many of his initiatives continue to flourish to this day. In temperament he was mercurial. There were occasions when he tried to be affable, at other times he would not utter a word. In all my contacts with him I never heard him raise his voice. Annoyance was always expressed facially, not verbally. When he visited the parish he met each priest in private. He was interested in how you were doing. It was an occasion when you were gently brought to account if needed. There were certain things that were not negotiable – visitation of the houses of the people topped the list. On the occasion of Confirmation, he usually dined with the priests of the parish. They were happy occasions, but one always watched one's p's and q's in his presence. Once he came to confer Confirmation in Walkinstown. On alighting from his car, he went straight to the altar and vested for the ceremony. When all was over, the same happened, in reverse. Apart from the ritual, not a word was spoken to anyone. This wasn't usual.

The memory of John Charles McQuaid is rare in its uniformity. Here is what the late Fr Michael O'Carroll, CSSp had to say:

> It was just his appearance. He seemed to have an aura or atmosphere about him that was unusual. His features were finely chiselled, his bearing was reserved but full of dignity. Serenity and the sense of one living mostly within. A hint of mystery which scarcely declined through the vicissitudes of the intervening years.

Under John Charles McQuaid that wonderful film group *Radharc* was established. I am sure he was less than thrilled with some of the work they did, but was sufficiently astute to turn a blind eye to the innovative pastoral agenda they so subtly promulgated. The *Catholic Social Service Conference*, now *Crosscare*, tackled the problem of deprivation, at a time when the national coffers were bare. His realisation of the plight and pain of emigration was genuine, although I have no doubt that their spiritual rather than their physical welfare was a high priority. The *Catholic Youth Council* was a flourishing organisation. Well I recall the hundreds who attended seminars and conferences at Red Island Holiday Camp in Skerries in the 1970s. The *Institute for Adult Education* in Mountjoy Sq, now gone, was a very significant establishment for adult education at a time when few organisations provided a possibility for learning, especially for those people who left school after the Primary Certificate. The stamp of John Charles McQuaid is crafted deeply on the Diocese of Dublin and it will remain so well into the future.

Under the archbishop were minor potentates called Vicars General. Their power and influence was ubiquitous. They were the ones who gave permission for a wide variety of things. They presided at regular deanery meetings where the ordained clergy were regularly examined, in the presence of their confrères, on theological topics chosen in advance. Normally, clerics would give Vicars a wide berth and call on them only when needed.

From the lay side of the divide, the view was a bleak one. A number of eighty-year-olds with whom I spoke, told me that the stance of the laity towards the clergy in their youth was one of fear. 'Terrified,' one man claimed. Another said 'nervous and cautious'. If you passed a priest in the street without saluting him, you were pulled up and corrected on the spot. Failure to attend the monthly sodality resulted in the priest chasing the delinquent to find out the reasons for non-attendance. Men sat on one side of the church, women on the other. Any mingling of the sexes was weeded out before Mass began. Confession was a huge problem and engendered more fear than relief or healing. One elderly woman said to me that she 'felt sorry for priests and their sad lives'. However, most now feel that the pendulum has swung too far in the opposite direction and lack of any respect is the problem today.

In general, priests were hardworking and generous with their time and talents. They were zealous for the spiritual and temporal and spiritual welfare of their parishioners. In those early days, sick calls in the middle of the night were not unusual. Long hours in a stuffy confessional were a weekly experience.

The schools were visited. In each parish a priest was regularly on duty and easily available. The Divine Office was recited regularly. No whiff of clerical scandal ever drifted in my direction in my early priesthood.

What purpose was served by creating a cadre of clerics so radically different in training and outlook from the generality of the population? Were we medicine men capable of casting spells? Was the mystique part of the message? Why was it that the attitude of the people towards the priest was one of nervousness tinged by fear? I believe that the model of priesthood I have described may have served the people well in the past. A new model of priesthood is needed in a new age and culture. It is not necessary for the essential truths of the faith to be altered to construct a priesthood that will serve people in a more creative and innovative way. A focus of the present pontificate has been to reinforce the essential difference (a difference *in essence* according to the Pope) between priest and layperson. Recent Roman directives have been issued discouraging the priest from giving the 'sign of peace' to the laity at Mass for fear of a blurring of the distinctiveness of their position and role in the church.

> In many ways you're like an old man. Perhaps
> You walk alone more than most people twice your age
> You notice each change of weather, the drift
> Of smoke to sky. There is a certain decorum
> You follow in your dress, the way you comb your hair
>
> You may have many acquaintances, few friends;
> Besides your unreplying God you have no confidant.
> Nevertheless you lift your hat to all. Old ladies
> Especially will seek you out, sometimes a sinner
> You are guest at many celebrations, a must at birth or death

Sometimes you wonder whether this is how God intended it.' (Pádraig J Daly, *Irish Poetry of Faith and Doubt*, ed John F. Deane, Wolfhound Press)

There are powerful voices seeking a return to the past. Once I took a short car journey with Archbishop Dermot Ryan of Dublin in Rome. He remarked, nostalgically, on how wonderful it was to see all the nuns on the streets wearing their habits. I disagreed. To me, these immaculate, ethereal creatures, well fed and coiffed, witnessed to a world of security, of predictability, of safety. They would never have to confront the hazards and unpredictability of family life. Of being without. Of worrying about the future of children, or where the next meal was to come from. They were too precious for me, and my uneasiness led me to suggest to the archbishop that it would be much better if they wore lay clothes. He wasn't impressed. It wasn't a world I deep down wanted to belong to. A recent brief letter to *The Irish Times* read, 'Madam, I recently saw a priest in full clerical garb walking down Grafton St. Is this a record? Yours sincerely ...' What sort of person wrote this letter? Perhaps priests are less challenging, safer and sanitised, if they are kept apart from the rest of people!

Being a priest means choosing always to be different. One was branded, even in the family, as the priest. He was the one who would be available to baptise, marry and bury family members. One who would never really belong at the family table. Always an outsider.

American poet, Jessica Power writes in a beautiful poem, 'There is a Homelessness', about loneliness:

> It is, more even than homelessness of the heart,
> of being always a stranger at love's side ...
> it is the homelessness of the soul in the body sown;
> it is the loneliness of mystery.

Yes, that is what we lived – the loneliness of mystery. Families have a dynamic of intimacy which, understandably, excludes those who do not belong to the circle of the first degree. It is being outside the club that has its own concern and rules. I know single people, who never married, can also feel this subconscious exclusion.

So, this is how it all began nearly forty years ago now. Let's move on to a wider canvas.

CHAPTER NINE

The Parish

In the countryside, the parish wraps pride and passion together. The name of the townlands which comprise the parish are known by everyone. Even the fields are named. Photographs of local parish football and hurling teams, on faded dog-eared calendars, adorn the walls in the local pubs. The parish as church fits naturally in with a web of other activities. The names of priests past are easily recalled. Parishioners know each other's history. There are families who haven't talked to each other for generations. Perhaps a row over a scrap of land divided them years ago. There are others for whom the old half-door still is a symbol of hospitality and welcome. Even in rural parishes, a way of life is oozing away. But it has not gone completely. This is a vignette of a typical rural parish, Dysart, in Co Clare, celebrating Jubilee 2000:

> There was a real sense of history in Dysart on Sunday last, National Pilgrimage Day. Those on pilgrimage to the 12th century High Cross followed in the footsteps of the people who prayed at that hallowed spot over many years. The surroundings of Dysart Church and Graveyard, the beautiful, mature trees in full bloom, and the sun shining down on the gathering, brought out a feeling of well-being and goodwill in all who participated in the Pilgrimage.
> Almost every town land in the Parish was represented at the Devotions. After solo performances from Gary Shannon and Tara Breen, a figure of the Caledonian set was danced as the pilgrims gathered round the bonfire.
> Children from Toonagh and Ruan Schools displayed quotations from scripture and read Prayers of the Faithful. There was livestock to represent the goats which will be sent to families in Africa, as part of the local Jubilee 2000 celebrations. The local guild of the ICA was on hand to share out

refreshments. Fr Tom Burke paid tribute to the Parish Council and all who were involved in making the day such a wonderful success and he also thanked Brendan and Nancy Keane, on whose land the High Cross stands, for allowing the Pilgrimage on their property. Finally, a beautiful Blue Cedar was planted in both Churchyards, as a reminder to future generations of what took place in the Parish on Sunday 21 May, 2000.

The car has ever so subtly driven people apart. The creamery, once a place of fraternity, is gone. House dances and story-telling have fast disappeared. Even the annual Pattern Day (Patron's day) has faded into memory. But, all this is strange territory for many urban dwellers. In the vast conurbations of ticky-tacky housing estates, the parish for many is no more than the building in which they may or may not worship on Sundays. For others, it is a vague geographical area, which happens to have a church. Their children are baptised there, and it is the place to which they will brought when they die. They are unlikely to know the names of the priests, and they do not foresee any need for a deeper relationship with the parish or priests. Their occasional visits to the church are for the funeral of a neighbour, or to obtain a certificate either of Baptism or Confirmation. But, in every geographical area known as a parish, there is a significant cluster of people for whom the parish is a vital, life-giving organ of spiritual energy. There are still those who live an intense Catholic spiritual life, and are willing to give committed service to their parish.

For a person steeped in the language of church, the parish is not principally a structure, a territory or a building. It is the Family of God in this particular place. It is a fellowship, a community, a home. It is, above all a Eucharistic community – where people gather to worship and praise God, to give thanks and to intercede for their needs and the needs of the world. The parish is the church situated in this neighbourhood. Its way is to be deeply inserted in human society and intimately bound up with its aspirations and with the dramatic events of their lives. In September 1966 I received a letter from Archbishop McQuaid. The terse one-liner read, 'I have pleasure appointing you to

Walkinstown Parish. Please contact the Parish Priest, Fr James Flood, to make the necessary arrangements to take up your appointment on Saturday 29 June. I wish you well in your new appointment.' The date was the following Saturday. The location of Walkinstown was a complete mystery to me. I had six days to pack my bags and leave Rathmines, where I had been chaplain to St Louis Convent. For two years I lived in dingy bed-sitters and for a few months in 'digs'.

Walkinstown was a huge conurbation of mixed housing in the western suburbs of Dublin. The neighbouring parishes were Crumlin, from which it was established, and Drimnagh. I was appointed as a Reader. A Reader was the lowest form of clerical life. I was on a fixed salary of £10 a week. The Reader, whose status was lower than that of a curate, propped up the whole worldwide clerical hierarchy, right up to the Pope. I arrived to be told, 'We have found "digs" for you with Mrs Conole in Landsdown Valley.' After a year in a dingy hovel of a bed-sitter in Brighton Square in Rathmines, I dug my heels in. The senior curate, Fr Pat Corriden, who lived in a fine, four-bed roomed house, relented or had compassion on me, and took me in. It was a lonely beginning.

The happiest day of my priesthood were spent in Walkinstown. There were nearly twelve hundred houses in the area of the parish for which I had responsibility. I grew to know and appreciate a lot of people. Each priest was attached to the many religious and secular groups in the parish. We had such fun. One family, the Garveys, had regular 'seisiúns' in their home. We sang and danced and rejoiced in the gift of friendship. I joined the GAA Club, Naomh Gearóid's, and played a few games for them. A few of us had regular games of poker in the houses of parishioners. I joined Newlands Golf Club at a time when it was still known as the 'Busman's Club'. I was a reasonably good golfer then. The wonderful companionship of the club member was a great support. The friendly atmosphere in the club made Newlands a home-from-home.

For many Catholics today the parish *is* the church. It is the place where things happen, spiritually, for them. Just as the local supermarket is the place for shopping, and the larger company with its myriad of branches nationwide is important, so the parish is the place where there is the some sense of belonging. The Vatican with its multiplicity of Congregations and Offices is only of relative importance to any Catholic. The bishop might easily acquire an inflated idea of his importance. He might be surprised to learn that in a large diocese his name does not trip too easily off the tongue of the person in the pew.

> 'People will enter into the mysterious rhythms of birth, marriage, sickness and death, vis-à-vis the parish. The impression that the parish community makes at these archetypal times will be lasting. It will be a critical factor in the subconscious appreciation of the church's mission. For all so involved, Catholic and non-Catholic alike, the parish will form a lasting impression of what they think "the church" is all about.'

The parish is important. The United States Bishops, in a 1993 document, opened like this:

> The parish is where the church lives. Parishes are communities of faith, of action, and of hope. They are where the gospel is proclaimed and celebrated, where believers are formed and sent to renew the earth. Parishes are the place where God's people meet Jesus in world and sacrament and come in touch with the source of the church's life.

The parish is still the place where the church lives. It is where the milestones of life are celebrated by most of those who still proclaim themselves to be Catholic. It is the place where I become a member of a worldwide, spiritual family, tracing its lineage right back to its founder, Jesus Christ. Long after some cease attending church, it is still fondly remembered. As a workman on a church building project was anxious and proud to tell me recently, 'This is the place where I was baptised and made my First Communion.'

As I travelled in various parts of the world, the similarity between parishes gave one a grasp of the universality of the church. In Gordonville, five miles south of Cairns in Queensland, Australia, where I once gave a parish mission, the similarities with any Irish parish were far more profound than any differences. The problems of recruiting people for ministry, caring for the sick and trying to reach out to the lapsed and un-churched, were analogous to the Irish situation. In São Paulo, I saw small bible groups in deep discussion in a large parochial hall. The same could be happening in big and small parishes anywhere the sun rises. I recall a visit to Bombay and being asked to offer Mass before I had time to put my head on the pillow. Some of the hymns we sang that night had been used at my last Mass in Dublin, prior to my departure. The parish is not a branch office of the diocese, nor is it a simple subdivision of the worldwide Catholic Church. It has its own dynamic, life, mission, and its own identifiable faith community.

Communication is at the heart of what the Church is all about. The parish exists to bring people into communication with God and, thereby, open them up to communication with each other. First century Christians would have wondered about expressions like, 'I'll meet you in front of the church,' or 'Is the church fireproof?' The building where these early Christians met was not the primary focus of their concern – the church was the assembly, the people, the community of faith. The community pre-existed the provision of the building. We probably have that first century experience when we celebrate Mass in a private house, surrounded by family and friends. On occasions like that, we have a palpable sense of community and church in the people gathered. At such celebrations, we instinctively know the environment to be right.

After Walkinstown, I was out of parish ministry for almost twenty-five years, and returning to a parish after all that time years was traumatic. Holy Family Parish, Kill of the Grange, is sandwiched between its more affluent neighbouring parishes of Foxrock and Dún Laoghaire. It was carved out of adjoining parishes in 1972. Many of the older parishioners still retained their allegiance to their parish of origin.

I couldn't believe the small smattering of parishioners, many of the elderly, who came to Mass on that first Sunday. I had heard stories from fellow clerics about the drop in attendance, but I believed their tales were fanciful exaggerations.

I immediately set about determining the true state of religious practice. The following Sunday we had counters at all doors at every Mass. The reality was worse than my worst fears.

About 10% of the parishioners attended. Even allowing for another 10% who went to adjacent parishes, the result was very disappointing. I couldn't help asking myself, 'Where are we going to be ten years from now (2001)?' This was a time for listening, watching, and discerning in the company of others.

How do we build a parish community so that each recognises himself, or herself, as part of something greater? A congregation of individuals, who happen haphazardly to live in a particular geographic area adjacent to this particular building called church, is hardly a community. The main goal of the pastoral efforts of the church is to build communities which make it possible for a person to live a Christian life. St Paul talks about the purpose of Christianity when he tells us that we are 'no longer strangers and sojourners but you are fellow citizens with the saints and members of the household of God' (Eph 1). Effective worship, which is life-giving, is enhanced when it is a community that celebrates.

When I last ministered in Walkinstown, it was the parish community that gave many individuals a sense of belonging. From their Catholicity and their parish they received a clearly defined identity. Their patterns of relationships, outside of the immediate family, were frequently those forged within the parish community. The parish was a significant source of social capital. This is still the case in rural areas. Apart from people who are no longer churchgoers, more and more people are surfing from congregation to congregation. While they may be still religious, they are less committed to a particular community of believers. 'Believers' perhaps, but 'belongers', no. Catholics need to re-connect with each other in an individualistic, competitive world. This is what the parish exists to do – build a community of believers who live out an inter-relationship with one another.

The average parishioner in the parish comes to Mass only on Sunday. Apart from Mass and, perhaps, an occasional penitential service, the vast majority have no other contact with the parish. When this parishioner comes to Mass, he find himself in a church filled with people he does not know for the most part, and in a different group from the last group he went to Mass with the previous Sunday. The Mass he attends is 'standard' for that Sunday. At Mass, this parishioner rarely knows the person sitting next to him unless it is a member of his own family or a near neighbour. There is little interaction among the congregation. Our parishioner knows a number of other people in the parish but he knows them, not because they are parishioners, but because they are his neighbour, his barber, his doctor, and his postman. In other words, they happen to be people he knows from another source and who also happen to go to this parish. The parish, then, is primarily a service institution, providing Mass and the sacraments for those who come. Even the clerical leadership in the parish is transitory. Others who have been through the seminary and have been ordained can replace them. The people who work in various ways in the parish form another group. They are the main source of parish activities. Those who work together may know each other. They are a recognisable environment, but not a very strong one. The average parishioner is not one of them.

Some months ago, I received a funny, peculiar letter from a young man who attended two churches of different Christian denominations, one Roman Catholic, the other Anglican. His reasons for doing so epitomise the strong community dimension of the Anglican Communion and what is lacking in the average Roman Catholic parish.

This story has a powerful message for Roman Catholic parishes everywhere. I am reproducing it in full, with the permission of the author, in the hope that it will inspire priests and people to build communities that are open, encouraging, and supportive to faith.

> I am often asked why, as an active member of my local Catholic parish, I also attend an Anglican Church each Sunday. The following may help explain.
> In 1993, I returned from seventeen years in India and was very disappointed to find church life in Dublin very dull and uninspiring in contrast to the vibrant spirit-filled groups I had enjoyed here in the early seventies.
> In 1994, I went to hear a visiting Canadian speaker at an evening service in an Anglican Church. I found the congregation of mainly 20-40 year olds very enthusiastic and encour-

aging. In particular, I was attracted by the strong singing of those present. I love singing but find it difficult to keep in tune unless there are strong male voices around me to carry me along. This was one of the few churches where I found such singing. It was a major attraction for me. After some months of regular attendance I made a number of friends. These were people who had similar interests to me. They were seeking to live a holy life. They were interested in prayer and the bible and ready to discuss spiritual issues. I was invited to meals and parties in the homes of people,. I was invited to join groups going hill walking, BBQs etc. After my years in India I had few Irish friends and this offered me a new social life away from the pub culture and night clubs. One couple who live near me offered me a lift home and in time invited me to join a small group on Wednesdays in their house where we prayed together and discussed the bible and questions of faith.

All this time I continued as a daily communicant, a practice I developed in my teens. My Sunday and Wednesday evenings were added extras to my usual Catholic practices. I informed my parish priest that I was attending these meetings and I also informed the Anglican minister that I was attending his church as a visiting Catholic. Both seemed content with this. Within a few months of my attending the Anglican parish I was invited to be involved in the various ministries and activities of the Church, such as praying with those who ask for prayer, running courses such as Alpha etc. I felt I was making a contribution to the group. If I missed a week, I was missed and told so by many the following week. In a way I felt I was part of the group putting on the show, rather than the audience looking on. I had been encouraged to read the Vatican Council documents encouraging greater lay participation in the church, but it seems so difficult to implement this, almost forty years later. In 1998 I suffered a serious illness and was hospitalised for four months. During this time I and my family were supported and visited by my friends from the Anglican Church as was usual when any member was in difficulty. This was in marked contrast to the Catholic parishioners where it was not the custom to organise such support.

In summary, as well as continuing my involvement in my local Catholic parish, I attend the Anglican Church because the members are enthusiastic in living out their faith and support me in my attempts to do so. I can see no reason why the same model could not operate within the Catholic Church and am saddened that so few seem interested in even considering this, particularly as there are not many 20-40 year olds active in the average Catholic parish.

Overall it may be said that I am a practising Catholic because I find the prayer and the sacramental structures help me in my private relationship with God, but in the Anglican parish I experience the support and challenge of being in a community living our response to the gospel together'

Our first effort in my new parish were directed towards the building once more of community. The church should be restructured to form basic Christian communities. For most people this community will be the parish. There is a tendency to think that structural renewal and institutional renewal is the same thing. Few people think in terms of environmental (or communal) renewal. It is rare enough for people to ask the basic question: 'How can a Christian environment (a Christian community) be formed most effectively?' The same problem can be looked at from a different point of view. The goal of the church is not to have structures, but to have people who are living as Christians.

In theory, the parish is the basic Christian community. It is supposed to be the smallest pastoral unit in the church, the ordinary place in which a person's Christian life can be nourished. Yet, it is clear that most parishes as we know them are not such places. This is partly because of their size, partly because of the way they are structured. A major problem in dealing with parish renewal is that we do not tend to think much in environmental or in communal terms. This struck me forcibly on my first Christmas in my present parish. The Monday night collectors and the weekly count people were having a little party in the sacristy room. In the very next room, members of the choir were having their pre-Christmas celebration. Not only were they apart, but I discovered they hardly knew one another. Apart from a few exceptions, they didn't know each other by

THE PARISH

name. What appeared from the outside very much like a community of sorts, were in fact groups of good, committed people who saw their primary role as one of service in a particular area.

Frequently, the word communion is used in a purely functional way. We could talk about the hospital as a community. Credit Union members are in some loose way a community. So is the Irish Farmers Association. But, these are functional communities. People come together to do specific tasks. In such a community, people relate in a task-orientated manner. The vision of a Christian community is more than functional. It is an environment.

A person's beliefs, attitudes, values and behaviour patterns are formed, to a great degree, by his environment and, therefore, the normal person needs a Christian environment if he or she is going to live Christianity in a vital way. A family is an environment, as is a group of friends. A school provides a place for environment to form, as does a parish or a business. There are usually a number of environments in a person's life – the family, work, recreation, the group of friends he or she spends time with. An environment is formed when a group of people interrelate or interact with some measure of continuity and stability. For an environment to be Christian, Christianity has to be a strong, influencing factor in the way people in the environment interact. In other words, the people share a common belief, place a premium on the common values that underpin their beliefs, and interact out of their faith. A stranger wandering into a truly Catholic parish environment would immediately sense that there was something different here. In the present arrangement, the Roman Rite is designed to help the people who have come together in one place to become a unified assembly, to realise that they are with their brothers and sisters, and that Jesus is present among them.

I quickly learned, as a first principle, 'assume nothing'. For instance, I assumed that the good people who attended the daily ten o'clock morning Mass knew one another, certainly by sight, but probably also by name. We invited the congregations of the morning Mass to the Parish Resource Centre for tea or coffee after Mass one day. What seemed to me a very homogeneous group of like-minded people was, in fact, a collection of individuals. One lady told me she had been attending the ten o'clock Mass since the church was opened and hadn't made friends with anyone. This reinforced my view that the energies of the parish ought to be invested in fostering the growth of community as a first priority. Everything else, including a life-giving liturgy, is very dependent on the health of the parish as a community. Despite Vatican Two, we still have a very privatised type of religion.

One of the first decisions we took in Kill of the Grange, my new parish, was to establish a team of greeters. From my work with New Religion Movements, I knew that many people are attracted to these movements because of their need to belong; a need for a sense of community. Many people need to come to terms with themselves, to feel safe, secure, and be able to overcome complexes. In addition, most assumed that 'nothing happens at Mass'. How could we indicate gently that we wanted to be that sort of community? Many years ago a young person said to me, 'Nobody would miss me if I didn't go to Mass.' I knew that what she said was true. At two of the principle Masses on a Sunday, our team of greeters were available at each door of the church to welcome people and offer them the parish newsletter. It was a small gesture. Many of the parishioners were elderly and they appreciated a word of welcome and a gesture of kindness. The greeters came to know the congregation, and the genuine welcome parishioners and visitors received was very much appreciated. There is more community in a pub than in a church!

Because of the privatised nature of religion, there is a fear of others in church. Did you ever notice how many people sit at the edge of the pew? Others will deliberately choose a seat apart from others. The sign of peace can be done very perfunctorily – a gesture that avoids eye contact at all costs.

Our second decision was to initiate, a 'Doughnut Sunday' on the first Sunday of every month. After Mass, in the large hospitality area at the back of the church, the congregation gathered for chat and refreshments. Again, it was a small gesture, an effort to recreate a sense of family, of belonging. Probably only half of the congregation remained behind to fraternise. After more than a year, people were still shy of making contact with strangers. In big cities, unfortunately, many of our congregations are just that – strangers to each other. Yet Irish people are known universally for their friendliness. In the past, the stress on the performance of one's duty robbed the assembly on Sunday. And yet, every rural church congregation spent considerable time together, standing around after Mass discussing crops, the weather, football or hurling. The connection between the church and what went on in it, and the real tight-knit community that actually existed may have been implicit, but was rarely articulated.

If I say liturgy – what comes into your mind? Perhaps actions, symbols, music and words? But something needs to happen first – the building of community. When a parish team meeting takes place, it will regularly concern itself with scheduling Masses, repairing buildings, getting readers and commentators, organising collections. It will consider these important, because it is assumed that every parish must have certain activities. The function of those in charge of the parish is to see that these activities happen. It is sometimes assumed, in fact, that the more activities a parish has, the better a parish is. A priest, at least, was given certain skills to perform certain activities well. Our practical training was activity orientated. There is a competitive streak in many priests who multiply activities and, thereby, generate kudos for themselves and their parish. There may be a buzz among the few who are excited and energised by parochial activities. Our vision of community must be broader, to embrace even the disaffected.

With only 10% of the parish attending Sunday Mass, and very few young people in sight, there were adequate reasons to be despondent at times. There were times when we only saw the way things were, not the way they might be. I know this is the ultimate blindness. This kind of blindness has nothing to do with sight; it has to do with lack of vision, and vision is the stuff of dreams, hopes, and possibilities. There is always the temptation to scale down our dreams to the size of our fears, until our vision becomes so tunnelled that we see darkness everywhere. I read somewhere that a 'visionary is someone who sees in the dark'. There is a continuing temptation to sigh, 'What's the use, nothing seems to work.' The temptation is to settle for the service model of parish. People are under more pressure than twenty-two years ago. Two parent working families, daily traffic congestion, child-minding problems and a huge array of options for leisure or 'free' time, means that attracting people to ministry is more difficult. Those who tend to volunteer are, normally, from the older age group, who have fewer pressures and less responsibility to attend to. Few enough people ask themselves the question, 'Where will our parish be ten/twenty years down the line?' When a person tells me, 'We tried that before' as a reason for not trying it again, I tend to lose heart.

We decided to organise a Ministry Sunday. Looking at the age profile and numbers of people at Sunday Mass, the question had to be faced – will our parish survive? It was not beyond the bounds of possibility that this large building would become a massive carpet sales room, or a spectacular theme pub, in ten or twenty years' time. The people were asked, 'Is this what you want?' They were invited to take ownership of the parish. All the ministries presently operating in the parish were listed and a few new possibilities added. People were invited, if they wished their parish to survive, to name an area best suited to their talents and to supply their names and addresses. This was completed after the homily of the Mass. Fifty five people, mainly Irish, but from five different countries, volunteered. We organised a meal for the volunteers. This was a 'getting-to-know-you' and a community building exercise. Just over half of those who volunteered attended the meal, which was a great success. Most of those who volunteered are now serving the parish in a variety of capacities.

We commissioned specially engraved crystal glass to present to long-serving parishioners. At a parish Christmas party, we presented these gifts to eight of the longest serving people in the parish. This small gesture created an enormous amount of good will and it provided one more opportunity for parishioners to come into contact with one another. One of our most successful initiatives was booking the local cinema and inviting parishioners to attend the film, *The Passion of the Christ*. We completely filled the cinema. After the film we returned to the parish for Mass, followed by refreshments and discussion groups on the film. There are signs that people are beginning to relate to one another in a new way. The journey is slow and the road is long.

The establishment of a 'gospel/story time' for pre-First Communion children, during the mid-day Mass on a Sunday. provided an opportunity for very young children to relate to the gospel in a way adapted to their age group and knowledge. A small team, led by our pastoral worker, developed this initiative over a year.

Don't be fooled by what appears impressive on paper. Everything we tried to do was nothing more than laying the foundations upon which the community could emerge in the future.

The creation of *communio* is the fundamental task of the church and the parish. The word 'communion' comes from the Latin *communio*, which comes from the Greek *koinonia*. We are most familiar with this word in relation to 'Holy Communion.' Communion designates a way of life, a network of relationships among churches and among individual Christians. Being part of a communion is a way of *being* – being in relationship with God and others.

In parochial work a sense of optimism, hope and vision are indispensable virtues. So much seems to be one step forward and two steps back, it is easily to become discouraged. In city parishes more and more people are 'shopping around'. Instead of a regular congregation that one can count on Sunday after Sunday, easy mobility means that one sees people on an 'on and off' basis. I notice that the numerical strength of the congregation varies from Sunday to Sunday.

CHAPTER TEN

The Dead and the Dying

My first parish, Walkinstown, was a huge, busy parish. It was there I first anointed a person (now known as the Sacrament of the Sick). I remember it well. In a tiny bedroom, the gaunt, emaciated face of a little old man gazed at me with pleading eyes. He moved in and out of consciousness. His face had a purple tinge. There was fear, hope and mystery in the encounter. He had nothing. I gave him a particle of the Eucharist – 'the bread of life.' I anointed his hands, forehead and feet, intoning the words, 'Through this holy anointing may the Lord in his love and mercy help you with the grace of the Holy Spirit ... may the Lord, who frees you from sin, save you and raise you up.'

This was the first time I had ever seen someone actually die. It moved me deeply. Death is a human trauma. It is a confrontation with mystery. Who am I Lord and who are you? Where am I going? The spirit left his body in one deep gasp and then nothing. Silence. In over forty years I have never grown used to death. Every death, both of the famous and the infamous, the rich and the poor, the possessed and the dispossessed, is traumatising. A whole history of a life lived, in who knows what circumstances, is gone forever from this earth. Who will remember? Death cuts the umbilical cord with one's family history, with friends, with places and memories. Death is a very profound mystery. Emily Dickinson has a poem that encapsulates these feelings around death:

> The bustle in a house
> The morning after death
> Is solemnest of industries
> Enacted upon earth –
> The sweeping up the heart
> And putting love away
> We shall not want to use again
> Until eternity

I find it impossible not to identify with the bereaved. The pain of loss is one of the deepest of all pains. With worldly things we can move objects around, we can change the configuration of events and agendas, we can make things better. In the face of death, we experience the frustration of helplessness. The wounds heal in time but the scars remain.

In twenty five years, I have discovered that the average parishioner no longer calls for the priest. I have officiated at funerals of those who have been dying over a period of time, without knowing. Afterwards, I am told, 'Ah, Father, we didn't want to frighten him' or 'We didn't want him to know that he was dying.' The deceased was given no choice. His or her freedom was taken away in the interests of a misguided compassion. To be helped to make the transition in union with Christ is surely the right of every Christian. Offering the possibility of spiritual help to a dying person is an act of love. The sacraments aren't magic. They are not designed to work miracles on those already dead.

It was in Walkinstown that I had my first experience of breaking news of the death of a loved one. I was never trained for that! A commercial traveller had a fatal accident on his way home from the country. His wife worked in premises on the Quays in Dublin. For reasons I cannot recall, I was the one to break the news to her. As I drove to the city, I practised what I would say. How should I begin? 'I am very sorry to have to tell you that ...' sounded trite and unconvincing. 'Did you hear any news ...?' In the end I prayed that the Holy Spirit would place on my lips the words that needed to be spoken. I cannot recall what I said, but I do remember the lady breaking down and crying hysterically. She clung to me and was inconsolable. Her face was contorted with anguish. This is a time for forgetting about dignity and protocol. I hugged her close so that she might experience the healing that comes from body warmth. It was a terrible scene.

On these two occasions I was convinced that Jesus was a hidden witness at both scenes. His heart too had been broken. I felt that he too recoiled from the ache that accompanies the pain of loss. I found it difficult to contemplate death without any faith. To me, nothing gives meaning to death, except faith.

On another occasion, I was called to the pitiful scene of a young child who drowned in her bath having being suffocated by the fumes of a gas fire. After a lapse of nearly forty years, I recall the words of the 33rd Psalm that came to me that night, 'The Lord is close to the broken-hearted and those whose spirit is crushed he will save.' The heart of Jesus, who himself had experienced torturous suffering, must bleed at the death of a young one. They are special, 'Suffer the little children to come to me …' There is a helplessness deeper than any other experience in the face of the death of a young child. Their potential evaporates unfilled. The cherished hopes of parents will never be realised. It's awful, and words are so inadequate when a young life is snuffed out unexpectedly.

Three times I have assisted on the occasion of a death by suicide. One was a deliberate overdose. The struggle had become too much. Each person has a breaking point. Like a taut elastic band, it is just that little bit of extra pressure that causes a life to snap. In many cases the mind is unhinged. I do not believe that this is always the case. Deliberate suicide, with a clear mind, is an act of selfishness. No matter how it happens, close relatives keep asking, 'Could I have done anything to prevent this happening?' They ask, 'Was it my fault?' The dead one has gone, those who remain continue to suffer.

The pain of loss is not confined to the bereaved through death. The pain of separation in marriage is devastating. Over the years, I have experienced the pain of 'the forgotten'. I can recall being asked to visit a husband who had left a wife and five beautiful children to set up house with a young girl nearly half his age. It took a lot of courage even to knock at the door of the dingy lodgings he now called home. I was amazed at his unconcern at the aching pain he had left behind. This was before women found a voice in the home. They just didn't have the language or vocabulary to express the intense frustration of living in a relationship that was sterile. In those far off days, feelings weren't named. They couldn't be. Later on in life, I was involved in a wonderful movement for people who have experienced the pain of loss through death, divorce or separation called The Beginning Experience.

Early on in my priesthood, the realisation dawned that

celibacy was going to be a problem. Here I was, in my early twenties, the hormones racing through my body, surrounded by so many pretty women. It is delusional to imagine that temptation wasn't a daily companion. Celibacy is experienced as a tearing apart of the human psyche from two directions. It is an ache that only occasionally dulls but never goes away. All the high minded spirituality and theology really doesn't make it any easier. Just as I was attracted to some of the women I met, I knew intuitively that, on a number of occasions, the attraction was mutual. I was unprepared for celibacy. Behind the closed wall of the seminary it is idealised and spiritualised. In the beginning, the physicality of the absence is gnawing. Later in life the lack of intimacy, companionship, deep friendship is, I believe, diminishing of the human person. It was around this time the first trickle of priests began to leave the active ministry. I would be a liar if I didn't confess that the option to leave was something I did consider on a number of occasions.

I loved what I was doing. I recall my sister Hilda once saying to me, 'The reason you like the priesthood is that people need you.'

CHAPTER ELEVEN

Sex Abuse

The most painful chapter in the church's history in Ireland is now being written under the glare of a frenzied mass media. The fall from grace of the church has left it severely debilitated, with a shattered morale. Gone is the 'cock of the hoop' self-confidence of the 60s and 70s. The old chutzpah has long disappeared. The Catholic Church has suffered a fall from grace akin to the toppling of the *ancien regime* in revolutionary France. The tremors of what has happened in the Irish church are being felt worldwide. The more than a million people who screamed their adulation of Pope John Paul in the Phoenix Park, Dublin on 29 September 1979 are silent and confused. Things will never be the same again.

As far back as I can remember, as a priest, there were always unsubstantiated rumours of priests who 'liked young boys' floating around. These stories were invariably second, third or even fourth hand, and they hung heavily on the clerical grapevine as a shadow without substance. Or so we thought. At times these alleged relationships were the stuff of smutty stories and sniggers. Occasionally a priest, with an obvious predilection for youngsters, was pointed out. His behaviour was noted, but nothing more than that. I don't think we really believed that there was anything untoward going on. Nevertheless, the peculiarity was remarked on.

In the seminary 'particular friendships' were heavily discouraged. It wasn't until I had left the seminary that I appreciated that this was to discourage any possibility of the emergence of a dormant homosexuality. At no time could we enter one another's room. Partners going to the university were regularly changed by the drawing up of a rota. I did hear a story of a priest being challenged by the father of a violated son, in the sacristy of a parish church. The man wanted the priest to take off his vestments and 'sort it out' outside. Again, this story had filtered through many mouths before it reached me. To be honest, I am convinced that the criminality of any such behaviour never even dawned on us.

I first heard the name Letterfrack in 1964. At the time, in Hollyfield Buildings in Rathmines, were living some of the toughest youngsters in the city. This territory later became the fiefdom of the full-time professional criminal, Martin Cahill, known as the General. Newly ordained, a chaplain at St Louis Convent, I was also involved in a youth club in Rathmines. I heard talk about comings and goings to and from Letterfrack. What was Letterfrack, I wondered? For the boys, to graduate from Letterfrack was to win an Oscar in undisputed toughness. It was an accolade they appeared to flaunt among their peers. They had a confident swagger about their walk. Who would dare square up to a Letterfrack graduate? The true 'hard man' title was one who had been to Letterfrack. This grim, forbidding place was the West Point or Sandhurst for street kids. In snatches of conversation, I soon learned that it was the Stalag One of industrial schools. The life was cruelly tough. It was a daily battle between the boys and the staff. I never heard any of the boys mention sex abuse as one of the cruelties inflicted on them. But then, they wouldn't have mentioned it to me. Their vocabulary would hardly have contained the words necessary to pass on the information in a credible way. As a very young priest, this was the first inkling I ever had that church personnel dealt in a cruel, harsh way with vulnerable delinquent boys.

It was nearly sixteen years later that I first reported a case of sex abuse by a priest to the diocesan authorities. I had received very trustworthy information that a priest of the diocese was consistently molesting young boys in a very serious way. I was shocked. Without consulting anyone, I immediately drove to Archbishop's House and reported the matter. I was contacted later and asked to make a verbal report to a Monsignor Richard Glennon, then the Parish Priest of Iona Road Parish. I knew intuitively that this was a deeply serious matter which had to be acted on immediately. Silence descended. I heard no more. To the best of my knowledge neither my informants, nor I, were ever contacted. I was deeply disappointed. I felt embarrassed whenever I meet my informants. I had nothing to report. I felt that they might not believe that I had even reported the matter. I began to avoid them even though they were friends of mine. To add insult to injury, the priest was still ministering. A long time afterwards, years I think, I was told informally that when challenged, the priest had denied everything. I wasn't recalled to substantiate my evidence. It was the priest's word over mine and I lost. This was bungling at the highest level, but my position as a relatively junior priest denied me the clout to pursue the matter, or so I thought. Maybe I was just a coward? At that time, in the late seventies, I wasn't aware that this was a criminal matter. Morally, I was conscious of the enormity of the offence, but that was all. Despite knowing that I was dealing with a serious moral issue, I was unaware of the depth of the trauma that such an experience inflicted on a young person. In my naïveté I thought that although this was a serious incident, the youngster would soon recover, as he would from a severe spanking from his father.

In one of the Jesuit schools I attended, I personally experienced an incident that was certainly mild sex abuse by a priest staff member. It lasted for over an hour and was accompanied by affectionate baby-talk. My trousers were removed, as a prelude to punishment, by a leering cleric who insisted that I sit on his knee. He obviously got his kicks from undressing young students in a sexually provocative way. It was only years afterward, when I was well into adulthood, that I fully appreciated what had happened to me. At the time authority figures could do no wrong. It was impossible to put shape or meaning on this behaviour, and it certainly wasn't something that I would dream of mentioning at home.

There was a second occasion on which I reported a case of clerical sex abuse by a priest working in the diocese. The allegations of abuse against this priest were fairly common knowledge in the parish. The parish was divided. Were the allegations true? Some believed they weren't. I rang one of the bishops to report what had been told to me. Once more this resulted in a deadly silence. I heard no more. The victim or his parents were never invited to substantiate the allegations. Both cases ultimately resulted in Garda interest and charges being laid against these two priests.

Undoubtedly there was, and perhaps still is, a peculiar ambivalence about clerical sex abuse among the clergy. The abusers were never considered evil ogres worthy only of condemnation. In fact, at least in one case, a known abuser was comforted by his clerical colleagues, who continued to select him on a clerical golf team and even to contribute to his club subscription. I assume the reason for the ambivalence is the hope of repentance. Don't isolate the sinner. He can change. There is also the notion that love is peace at any price. To call anyone to account for his behaviour was considered an unloving act. Up to very recent times, I can never recall a priest being sacked. A priest ploughs an individualistic furrow, accountable to no one. There are priests who in spite of everything that has happened, defend the church with a robustness that is frightening. Their arguments fly in the face of the available evidence. There is still a deep-seated attitude of denial in many church quarters. The Catholic Church has the capacity to capture the intellect, to the extent that it can do no wrong.

The majority of people are baffled at the negligence of church leadership in the face of child abuse. Priests were moved from parish to parish. Some were ordered to therapy centres to be 'cured'. This was a strategy for which the psychiatrists must bear some of the blame. Medical personnel often gave offenders a clean bill of health for further ministry. There were times when moving an offending priest from parish to parish was not solely the decision of the local bishop. Sex abuse, at least initially, was viewed primarily as a moral problem – a serious lapse from grace. The remedy was repentance, a period on retreat and spiritual rehabilitation.

Celibacy is a strange land. It isolates a person from the cutting edge of pain. For a cleric, consideration for the victim is not unlike watching the spectral images of the hungry on television. Sad, even disgraceful, but not a pain that reaches the gut. Married people can speculate – what if my child was savagely violated? A father or mother can feel, with a depth of emotion, the wrenching pain of having a son or daughter abused. A cleric cannot understand that sort of pain. No matter how much a cleric wants to be compassionate, the profoundness of his feelings can never reach that of a parent. Celibacy isolates. The begetting and rearing of children is a primal experience at the epicentre of what it means to be human. A celibate cannot replicate the nurturing instinct of a parent. Yet, celibacy is an issue which the church is unwilling to consider. In addition, the absence of the feminine face at a leadership level in the church is to deprive it of the intimacy and insights that are unique to women. Is it any wonder that Jesus surrounded himself with ministering women and chose a married man to be the first Pope?

My fourth experience in the realm of clerical sex abuse caused me the most disappointment. Nearly fifteen years ago I had a phone call from a bishop asking me to consider finding a vacancy for a priest of his diocese. I agreed to meet the man. Within minutes, I felt very uncomfortable in this priest's presence. He treated me to excessive flattery, interspersed with a spurious account of his own competence. He was a strange man, overweight, wearing dark glasses, with deviousness in his countenance. I told him no position was available. Despite this, he wangled his way, uninvited, into the Communications Centre, for which I was responsible. The media later claimed he raped a young person on my watch. I don't think that was true. Whether it is true or not, I have no way of knowing. The deeply sad aspect of the story is that the priest, Sean Fortune, committed suicide before he could be brought to trial. Despite the fact that this man had a known background as a serial abuser, I was not informed. How could this happen? Was it an exaggerated notion of confidentiality? What is more important, the well being of young people or the keeping of confidentiality that ought to have been in the public domain?

It is hard to reach any conclusion, other than the bishops were simply out of their depth. The sort of vigilance that appears to the average person sound common sense, in terms of childcare and protection, did not seem to occur to our bishops. Men who are eternally vigilant in doctrinal matters failed lamentably in their duty of care to the vulnerable. When I was in publishing, I can recall haggling for half an hour with Archbishop McNamara over a sentence in a sex education book – he wanted to change 'a hug and a kiss' into 'a hug and a light kiss'. His conscience in this area was ever so tender. Yet, I have been informed that he changed a known abuser from one parish to another, despite protests from a senior priest of the diocese. On one occasion a very significant number of books were shredded in Veritas because of a trivial doctrinal error, again at the behest of Archbishop McNamara. This was at a time when priests were abusing young boys. How did we manage to lose the plot so seriously? The paradox is that bishops, like Archbishop McNamara, were essentially good men. I have no doubt they said their prayers and lived a modest lifestyle, but something, I know not what, dimmed their vision and discernment. Just like selective inattention, when we hear only what we want to hear, they had the capacity to disassociate from the unpalatable.

The church was ill-equipped to deal with the frenetic fallout from the clerical abuse scandals. It hadn't any PR expertise. Relations with the media were frosty. Trained personnel available to present the church's point of view simply weren't there. The church was wrong-footed when RTE, in its *Prime Time* special of autumn 2002, *Cardinal Sins*, went after Cardinal Connell. There was an inability even to correct the obvious faults in the programme. We failed to respond adequately, with our misguided idea of confidentiality, and by allowing every response to be driven by lawyers. Like a guilty child caught with its hand in the biscuit tin, we stuttered to give any coherent explanation of what was happening. The diocesan clergy were appalled and disappointed at the poor PR skills of the administration.

The wounds are still too raw to properly assess the effects of the sex abuse scandals on the clergy. Priests told me they were fearful of opening the morning newspaper for fear of another revelation. The same cases were rehashed, time and time again, in the newspapers. Every remand of an accused priest meant a full retelling of the original story. This naturally gave the impression to the media-consuming public that, as one religious correspondent put it, there was 'a flood of abusing priests'. Priests deeply resented the labelling of accused as paedophile-priests, when such a tag was not applied to any other profession. It was a sombre, dark time, to be a priest. One colleague described being followed by a group of youngsters in his parish, who called out 'Mister, are you a priest?' A raucous chorus of 'Paedophile! Paedophile! Paedophile!' followed his answer in the affirmative. Another priest friend told me that a man in the city centre spat at his feet, accompanying his action with a string of expletives. Some priests found it hard to leave the presbytery and avoided contact with people. Many would not wear their Roman collars, except in the parish, where they were known. Some withdrew, consciously and deliberately, from any contact with children. All spontaneity and naturalness in relation to children was quenched. A dark, threatening cloud hung over us clergy. We were conscious that people were probably questioning themselves, 'I wonder is he one of them?' I am sure even our own family members must have struggled with the same question. The 'how' and the 'why' of clerical abuse left us shocked and unnerved. There was also confusion in relation to what had happened in our midst.

I work in a diocese with over seven hundred priests in the direct employment of the diocese. We have no human resource person available for consultation or help. Letters from Archbishop's House either arrived to the parishes too late, or were unhelpful. As they struggled to deal with the massive fall-out, priests were left to themselves, to fly by the seat of their pants. Gradually, some leadership response was organised. The priests were briefed by the diocese about the extent of the problem and the steps being taken to deal adequately and compassionately with it. Some of us just couldn't understand how the victims were not the first focus and the principal concern of those in authority. The voices of the victims began to be heard. The National Conference of Priests took the initiative to initiate a forum where those who had been abused by clergy could tell their stories. The horror of the devastation wrecked on the personal lives of good, young people by clergy gradually began to be understood a little better.